Young People's Problems

Young People's Problems
Help and Hope for Today's Teenager

James Russell Miller

Solid Ground Christian Books
Birmingham, Alabama USA

Solid Ground Christian Books
715 Oak Grove Road
Homewood AL 35209
205-443-0311
sgcb@charter.net
www.solid-ground-books.com

Young People's Problems
Help and Hope for Today's Teen

James Russell Miller (1840-1912)

Taken from 1898 edition by Thomas V. Crowell & Co., NY

Solid Ground Classic Reprints

First printing in May of 2008

Cover work by Borgo Design, Tuscaloosa, AL
Contact them at borgogirl@bellsouth.net

ISBN: 978-1-59925-158-5

PREFATORY NOTE.

THE most important of all lessons are those which teach us how to live. There come points and experiences in every young person's life when a word may give help, save from mistake, and make the way plain and clear. It is in the hope of throwing light on some of the questions which are sure to arise in young people's lives, that these chapters have been written. It is not claimed that all the "problems" are here considered; but perhaps those eager to make life beautiful and rich will find a little help in some of these pages.

J. R. M.

CONTENTS.

CHAPTER		PAGE
I.	Helping with the Problems	7
II.	What am I here for?	13
III.	The Home Relation	20
IV.	About your Mother	27
V.	About your Father	34
VI.	About your Friends	40
VII.	Beginning a Christian Life	48
VIII.	Getting acquainted with Christ	55
IX.	About Consecration	62
X.	About Prayer	70
XI.	The Bible in the Closet	78
XII.	The Matter of Conversation	83
XIII.	On keeping Quiet	92
XIV.	Learning to be Thoughtful	100
XV.	On the Control of Temper	107
XVI.	Getting along with People	115
XVII.	The Matter of Social Duties	124
XVIII.	The Use of Time	132

CONTENTS.

CHAPTER		PAGE
XIX.	THE MAKING OF A MAN	139
XX.	ON KEEPING UP THE IDEAL	146
XXI.	A HIGH SENSE OF HONOR	153
XXII.	ON DOING OUR BEST	159
XXIII.	ABOUT YOUR SHADOW	165
XXIV.	YOUR LITTLE BROTHER	173
XXV.	THE BLESSING OF WORK	179
XXVI.	A GIRL'S QUESTIONS	186
XXVII.	WHAT IS THE COMFORT?	194
XXVIII.	LEARNING CONTENTMENT	201

YOUNG PEOPLE'S PROBLEMS.

CHAPTER I.

HELPING WITH THE PROBLEMS.

EARNEST young people have many problems. Life is all new to them. It is a voyage over new seas. It is a pilgrimage through a new country. At every point they are reminded, "Ye have not passed this way heretofore." Every day brings its new questions. At every step a new mystery arises, and they cannot rest until it has been solved for them. They are continually seeing things they have never before seen, and each new thing holds a new problem for them. They are meeting experiences through which they have never before passed; and they long to understand the meaning of them, and to know how to meet them.

The world seems familiar and commonplace to some who have been in it for a long time;

but it is a world of exhaustless wonders to the young, whose hearts are alive and whose minds are alert. A child that asks no questions is not a normal child; questions are signs of mental health and activity. A young person with no problems is either too dull of mind to be moved by anything beautiful or new, or too indolent to think or to try to answer the questions that evermore arise.

Young people's problems cover the whole of life. Beginning with the child's eager, curious questions about everything, they include the most serious matters of existence. What am I? Where did I come from? Where am I going? What am I in this world for? What shall I do with my life? How shall I treat other people? What are my relations to God? How shall I endure temptation, and contend against the evil influences which surround me on every hand? How can I grow into sweetness and beauty of character?

These, and a thousand questions like these, are forever arising in the mind of the earnest, thoughtful young man and young woman. They are questions, too, which should be answered. The very life depends upon finding the right answers.

No more important service can be rendered

to young people than wise help in meeting and answering life's questions, great or small. It must indeed be wise help, to be valuable,—else it were better not to try to help at all. Bad advice has wrecked many destinies. It is important that those who are set for the guidance of the young shall themselves know well the way, and shall be able to give wise counsel to such as seek it of them. Happy are the young people who are in natural, familiar relations with older friends of tried experience and sound judgment, who are able to answer their questions, to throw light upon their perplexing problems, and to guide them wisely in this world's tangled paths. Many go down in defeat and failure for the want of such true and safe help.

One of the dangers of such friendship, however, is too much advice. No doubt some young people are sorely hurt in this way. The very gentleness of the love that watches over them becomes a peril to them. One of the mistakes of home-life in many families is too much government. The best way to help the young is not to solve their problems for them, but thoughtfully to help them to consider and answer their own questions. When a child brings home from school a hard example in arithmetic, the worst help is to work the example for him. The same is true of all difficulties and perplexities of young persons. It is unkindness to them to do their thinking, choosing and deciding for them. It only makes them less able for meeting life's responsibilities when a little later they must face them alone, with no one who can give them counsel. Our best friend is not he who does the most things for us, but he who makes us self-reliant, who helps us to think and choose for ourselves, who inspires us ever to do our best. One of the tasks and tests of wise older friendship is self-restraint, self-repression, in the matter of advising and leading younger people. We are not to be dictators, but inspirers.

Of course, if we have had longer or wider experience, we have learned much about life and about the world, which should fit us for guiding others. But the help which others can get from our experience is limited. Really every one must learn his lesson for himself, from his own experience, must make his own experiments, must be taught by his own mistakes, must grow wise through his own reading, thinking, and living. Young people must, in the end, work out their own problems; and he is very foolish who, even in kindness of heart, tries to do it for them. Yet there is a way of giving them help which is wise and may do good. We may stimulate, encourage, suggest, cheer, strengthen, and thus make their lives nobler and richer.

In proposing to consider young people's problems, the writer has no thought of doing much more than help his readers to consider their own problems. Some of them probably fail to do even this. They seem not to realize that there are any problems in living. They never think below the surface of things. They are ruled by the present moment and by passing impulses and impressions. They have never learned to think through the questions which arise, but are content to let others think for them, or to follow blindly the moods of the passing experience.

For such as these the best service that can be given will be their awakening to the consciousness of the seriousness of life. For life is serious. We hear much said about how serious a thing it is to die; but really it is a much more serious thing to live. The dead are through with life's struggles; but for those who still remain in this world there must be continuous struggle, toil, and burden-bearing. Life is very serious, and should be met with earnest thought.

There are many young people, however, who already understand how important it is to give deep thought to life's questions, so as to make wise decisions and right choices. They wish to make the most they can of their life, to avoid mistakes, and to find the best things. Perhaps it may be possible to give true brotherly help to some of these, if not in the way of setting down specific directions, which it is not always practicable nor even desirable to do, at least by throwing a little light upon the path, which may make it somewhat plainer or clearer for their inexperienced feet.

The writer claims no special ability as an adviser of young people, and no particular right to their confidence, save that he has an earnest desire to help them find the right way, and is willing to tell them what he himself has learned in his own experience.

CHAPTER II.

WHAT AM I HERE FOR?

PERHAPS one of the earliest of young people's problems most frequently is, living itself. What am I in this world for? What should I do with my life? What was God's thought for me when he made me, and sent me here? How can I find out?

Frankly it must be confessed, however, that many young people do not ask these questions in any very definite form. Not many consciously take up the problems of life in such serious fashion as this. Nor would it be well if they were to do so. The most wholesome life is the least self-conscious. Too much introspection, looking in upon one's self, is not wise. Youth ought to be without care.

But while many do not consider life's great questions in any very definite way, every earnest young person thinks more or less seriously about what he will do with his life. He passes through a period of uncertainty and questioning before his mission becomes clear and plain to him. He has visions of beautiful things which he hopes some day to realize. He dreams dreams of the years before him, and sees himself achieving and attaining things which are honorable and worthy. But he has his days of deep thought, and sometimes of sore perplexity, before at last the goal appears shining before him, bright and unmistakable.

Much of this thinking is done for young people in their early years by those who have the direction of their training and education. Fortunate are they who have wise parents and good teachers, not who will decide for them, but who will give them proper direction and influence them aright. They have opportunities which others who are less favored lack. But whether they make anything worth while of their opportunities depends altogether upon themselves. Many young persons, with splendid privileges, do nothing with their life; while others, with everything against them at the beginning, grow into fine character and great usefulness. The difference is in the persons themselves, and in the way they take hold of life. Here is where the responsibility of young persons themselves comes in. What will they make of their opportunities? What will they bring out of their privileges?

WHAT AM I HERE FOR? 15

"What am I here for?" Your being here is no accident; there is divine design in it. God thought about you, and then made you, and sent you into the world for a purpose. There is a place he wants you to fill. There is a work he wants you to do. Something in the great divine plan for the world depends upon your filling your place and doing your work with fidelity. Other things will go wrong if you disappoint God by not fulfilling your mission. Even God will not do your work for you. It is a great step toward success to get deep into the heart the conviction that God has a plan for our life, something he made us to do. Goethe writes, —

What shap'st thou here at the world? 'tis shapen long ago;
The Maker shaped it, he thought it best even so;
Thy lot is appointed, go, follow its behest;
Thy way is begun, thou must walk, and not rest;
For sorrow and care cannot alter the case;
And running, not raging, will win thee the race.

How shall I learn what my mission is — what place God made me to fill, what bit of work is just my own? There really is nothing mysterious in this problem. No one need ever spend a moment in anxious questioning about it. There is a very easy way to find out what our mission is. If we simply do well the little duty of each day as it comes, we will be carrying out God's thought and plan for our life, and at the end will find that we have finished the work which God gave us to do.

No one must ever imagine that his mission is some fine, ethereal service, unlike any common work of common people. Most likely it is something very commonplace. The lowliest people, those who work in the humblest places, are sent of God just as truly as those who write immortal poems or sit on thrones.

Nor must you imagine that if God made you for some definite place and work, he will lift you into your place, and put the work into your hands in some supernatural way. God never did that for anybody. Even Jesus spent thirty years in diligent study and hard work, in preparation for the three years of wonderful ministry for which he was specially sent into the world. Whatever fine or distinguished thing you may have been born to do, you must be trained for it in the common days and in the common ways.

You must begin by being a diligent, dutiful child. Some of those who read these words are in school. School-life is important. Those who loiter over their lessons, or neglect, or miss them, are dropping stitches which some day will cause sad ravelling out. Napoleon, when once visiting his old school, said to the pupils, " Boys, remember that every hour wasted at school means a chance of misfortune in future life." Thousands of men and women have failed of their mission in life because they neglected their lessons in school.

Wellington said that the battle of Waterloo was won on the cricket-field at Eton. He meant that the training he had received there as a cricketer made him ready for fighting the great battle which decided so much for the world. We never can over-estimate the importance of preparation in the early days. All life depends upon it. Neglect then means failure by and by.

What young people are sent into the world to do now, in their youth, is to study, to work, to be faithful in lowly duty. What larger, greater task may come for them after a while they do not know, nor need they care to know. God's plan for them these happy days is unrelaxing diligence in the things that come to their hands. Doing these things well will train them for doing the greater things which the future may give them to do. Diligence in the school will fit them for places of responsibility in business.

Good cricket-playing will prepare them for winning victories on great battle-fields.

"What am I in this world for?" You are here to do God's will, and to fulfil his purpose for your life. This purpose he will make known to you, but only day by day, as you go on. If you do to-day's work, whatever it is, faithfully, as well as you can, that will be a little of God's will done, a fragment of God's plan for your life filled out; and then it will prepare you for doing next day's part of that plan when it is put into your hand.

There is an education, a building of character, going on in you all the while, even in the commonest, dullest, routine task-work. In the daily details of household tasks or office-work, you are learning patience, promptness, carefulness, diligence, power to endure. It may irk you to have to obey rules, to go always by the clock, to rise at the same hour every morning, to answer calls and bells; but out of this wearisome drudgery you will get the fine things of character which will make you strong, noble, rich-hearted, helpful to others, stable and secure for men to lean upon.

But remember always that you will never fill the place God made you to fill, nor do the work he has set down for you in his plan, unless you

WHAT AM I HERE FOR?

learn the lessons he appoints for you in the days of your youth. Wasted youthful days mean failure in life.

"The day has ended and the sun has set,
    Unfinished is the task I planned to do;
I sit and ponder o'er with deep regret
    The golden sunlight vanished from my view.

And thus full oft, at last, when life doth close,
    And toil is ended for the restless feet,
And for the busy hands the long repose,
    The cherished work of life is incomplete.

O Thou, who knowest all from sun to sun,
    From birthday morning to death's evening chill,
Look on thy children, with their tasks undone,
    In loving kindness, and forgive them still."

CHAPTER III.

THE HOME RELATION.

PERHAPS the home relation should present no problem for young people. It would not if homes were perfect. But the best homes on earth are only schools, with the lessons only partially learned. It is important that careful attention be given to these lessons now, for the opportunity to learn them will soon be gone. It is a serious misfortune for any one to go out from his home without having mastered the lessons which mean so much to him in preparation for life.

It is not always easy for young people to accept their place in the home, and adjust themselves to its limitations. It may as well be confessed frankly that the spirit of independence is usually strong in the breast of youth. Many young people chafe under the restraints of parental authority. They see no reason why they should submit. Some yield only after a struggle, and always with ill grace. Others do not yield at all, continually maintaining a spirit of rebellion, which mars the harmony and the happiness of the home, and leaves them undisciplined in character, and unready for the duties and responsibilities that await them when they leave the home door.

It should be clearly understood by all young people that parental authority is a divine ordinance. The Bible teaches that children shall submit themselves to their parents. One of the Ten Commandments expressly says, "Honor thy father and thy mother." To honor includes full and unquestioning obedience, while it implies also far more than mere formal obedience; it asks for love and respect, also homage.

Jesus set the example for all ideal human life, and the honor he gave to his home and to his parents is the example for all young people in their home. It was after he had had a vision of his higher relation to his Father in heaven that he went back with his parents to Nazareth, and continued subject to them. He found his heavenly Father's business for eighteen years longer in the lowly duties of the home relation. The submission of Jesus to parental authority and to home restraints shows that there is nothing unworthy in such subjection, but that, on the other hand, such recognition of authority is most fitting and beautiful.

The problem of the home relation is entirely solved in most instances when children have accepted their divinely appointed place in the family. Sometimes, however, there are special and peculiar conditions in a home which appear to young people themselves to make it impossible for them to live sweetly and happily in the relation in which they find themselves. Not all family government is ideal. There may be too much of the monarchical. Or there may be in the parents a lack of that self-mastery which is essential in those who would rule others well. Or there may be an utter absence of any true discipline — a home without government of any kind. Or there may be no religious life in the home; it may be thoroughly worldly, or even sinful.

In such cases the question may arise in the mind of a thoughtful young person who is trying to live worthily, "How can I do my part in the home where there is such failure on the part of others to do their part?" To this question the answer in general is, that no want of faithfulness in others can exempt us from the duty of being faithful, or change our duty in the slightest degree. One sin never excuses another. One's neglect of duty never absolves another from duty. You will do most toward correcting the faults or evils in your home by being all the more careful in your own life. If one member of the household is touchy, easily provoked, or is always saying or doing something to irritate the others, the way to make the very worst of the matter is for you to be like tinder, flashing up under every slightest provocation. The best way, however, to cure the fault in others is for you to be patient, forbearing, ready by fine tact to turn the opportunity for bitterness into humor — giving always the soft answer that turneth away wrath.

The art of living together, even within the sacred precincts of a home, is one that has to be learned; it does not come naturally. Home life is a splendid school for self-discipline. No one can have his own way altogether; there must be constant mutual concession. The young people of the household must learn that they, too, have to yield their preferences many times. Not only are there other people, but the other people are very close to them, and the law of love must ever hold sway in all the relations.

Young people usually have to learn to be thoughtful; thoughtfulness is not, in many persons at least, a natural grace. They are apt to speak out their feelings without thinking whom their words may hurt. They are apt to assert their rights without reference to the rights of others, and to follow their own hasty impulses without asking how their acts may affect those who are bound up with them in love's covenants.

The lesson of thoughtfulness well learned will solve many of the most serious problems of home life. Thoughtfulness includes the whole of the wonderful lesson of love taught by St. Paul in his immortal thirteenth chapter of First Corinthians. Love suffereth long and is kind. Love envieth not, vaunteth not itself, is not puffed up, doth not behave itself unseemly, seeketh not its own, is not provoked, taketh not account of evil, beareth all things, believeth all things, hopeth all things, endureth all things.

The lesson is put in another form in our Lord's life-motto: "Not to be ministered unto, but to minister." Any one who puts himself on a pedestal, a little throne, in the home, and demands attention, honor, homage, service, from the others, is going to be a serious troubler of the home life. Love's way is to seek not to be helped, but to help; not to be honored, but to honor; not to be waited upon, but to serve others in all loving ways. Those who have this aim pervading all their desire help to make the home life sweet and gentle. The spirit of serving is the spirit of Christ. We should train our hands to gentle ministries, our feet to errands of love, and our lips to encouraging speech.

The problem of the home-making is for the young people, the growing up or the grown-up children, quite as much as for the parents. They can mar all the beauty and all the good which the father and mother make with so much toil and care. One selfish son or daughter ofttimes destroys the peace and happiness of a whole household. On the other hand, one thoughtful, self-forgetful son or daughter may become the sweetener of the family life, sharing burdens, lightening cares, giving cheer, filling the house with song. Let the young people therefore accept their responsibility, and faithfully and gladly do their part in making the home. In trying to make happiness for others they will find the surest way of making happiness for themselves.

There is need for most careful thought on this subject. The home life is peculiarly sensitive to every influence from within. We do not seem ready to take as much from our own as we do from those outside. We are apt not to manifest the same self-control in our household relations that we do in our business life or our mere social relations. This very sensitiveness of the home hearts makes it all the more important that we should ever be exceedingly careful in all that we do and say within our own doors. Our own should get always the best we have to give. What one writes of Christian life in general is especially true of Christian life within the home doors : —

> The hands that do God's work are patient hands,
> And quick for toil, though folded oft in prayer;
> They do the unseen work they understand
>   And find — no matter where.
>
> The feet that follow his must be swift feet,
> For time is all too short, the way too long;
> Perchance they will be bruised, but falter not,
>   For love shall make them strong.
>
> The lips that speak God's words must learn to wear
> Silence and calm, although the pain be long;
> And, loving so the Master, learn to share
>   His agony and wrong.

CHAPTER IV.

ABOUT YOUR MOTHER.

SHE is the first friend you ever had. When you came into this great world as an utter stranger, not knowing any one, never having looked into any face, you found love waiting for you. Instantly you had a friend, a bosom to nestle in, an arm to encircle you, an eye to watch you, a hand to minister to your helplessness and need. Your mother received you eagerly, took you into her deepest heart, and began to live for you.

You never can know what you owe to your mother. It was a long while before you even knew what she was doing for you. In your helpless infancy she sheltered you and cared for you in unwearying patience and gentleness. She nursed you through your colics, your teething, your whooping-cough, your measles, and all the other ills which infancy is heir to. She walked the floors with you nights, trying to soothe your pains and quiet your bad tempers. She gave up her days to you, teaching you how to walk, how to talk, how to use your hands, your eyes, your ears, and giving you your first lessons in loving, in praying, and in everything beautiful.

You do not know, you never can know, all that your mother has done for you. It was not easy, either, for her to do it. She never complained, for love does not count the cost of its serving and sacrificing; but there was serious cost nevertheless. Some of the lines you see in her face these days are marks left by the toil and care which she gave so freely to you — price-marks of her unselfish love. Perhaps she is not so beautiful as she used to be — has wrinkles, and a tired look, and seems older, with more gray hairs. Not so beautiful? Ah, she is more beautiful just because of these lines and traces and furrows. They are love's handwriting. They are like the soldier's scars — honorable, because they tell what she has suffered, sacrificed, endured, for love of you.

Now, what about this mother of yours? Do you think you appreciate her at her true worth? Do you think you are returning to her in the worthiest way the love which she has lavished upon you through the years? Do you think you are proving yourself worthy of such unselfishness, such self-forgetfulness, such loving and serving unto the uttermost? It is very beautiful when a mother is old and feeble, or sick, to see her children ministering to her in sweet love, without thought of cost, without stint of sacrifice, doing all they can to comfort, bless, and brighten her old age. Often this picture is seen. When the children were in their infancy the mother's hands ministered to them in countless ways; now they are giving back a little of the love, paying a portion of the debt they owe to her. Heaven must look down with gladness upon such holy scenes.

But not all loving mothers are sick or infirm; sometimes they are strong and active, but lonely. Are you good to your mother when she is not an invalid? Some of us wait until our friends are sick before we show them the best that is in our heart. One said to-day — a sick woman — that she had never dreamed she had so many friends, or that they loved her so much, until she fell alarmingly ill — the doctor said she might not recover. Then the love poured out. Everybody she had ever known came to ask for her, and to express sympathy with her in her suffering, or to offer service.

This was very beautiful. But it would have been better if some of the love had been shown before, when she was well and strong, carrying burdens and dispensing good. It would have made life easier and sweeter for her. It would have put into her heart courage for even better and richer serving.

If your mother were to grow very sick to-morrow, there is nothing you would not do for her gladly and cheerfully. She would be most grateful to you, too, for your gentle kindness. But think how much of this ministry of love you might render now, though she is not sick. For example, you can give her your fullest confidence, and keep up a close and intimate friendship with her. Some young people drift away from their mother. They do not give her their heart's confidence as they used to do in their childhood. They hide things from her. They resent her questions when she would know about their companionships, their friendships, their pleasures, their plans of life.

It is a great comfort to a good mother to have her children confide in her, always telling her everything. Why should they not? Surely she has a right to know their most confidential affairs. The son, now a full-grown man, with heart and hands full, can give his mother no greater joy than by coming into her room every evening for a little confidential talk, just such as he used to have with her when he was a little fellow. The daughter, now a woman, need never be afraid to trust her mother with all the interests of her happy life. She needs the mother-counsel quite as much now as she did when she was a child, and the mother-heart craves the sweet confidence. We should never cease to be children to our mother. Nothing is more beautiful than such intimacy of children with a mother, even though the children be men and women in mid-life. To the mother they are always children, and their confidence is always sweet and sacred.

Another way you can return your mother's love, pay the debt you owe her, especially if you are a daughter, is by relieving her as much as possible of the care of the home and the housekeeping. Some daughters seem very thoughtless about this. The mother always has done everything — perhaps she has done her children harm in this very way. Some mothers are altogether too good to their children, make life too easy for them, bear too many of their burdens. It is mistaken kindness. Our best friend — the best mother — is one who makes us do what we can ourselves, thus training us to self-reliance. It were better for mothers to do as the eagle does with her young — make the nest rough for them, even push them out of it, that they may learn to use their own wings.

But no daughter, when she is old enough to think, should ever be content to let her mother continue to do for her, while she herself sits with folded hands, or runs the streets with her friends, or passes her time reading novels. She ought to determine to do her part, that her mother may have rest. It is not a picture which heaven can rejoice over, — a strong, healthy girl crimping, dressing, walking, reading, receiving, and calling, all the while; and her poor tired mother toiling, slaving, serving, in kitchen and living-room, cooking, sweeping, dusting, sewing, darning, until her strength is exhausted.

This is enough to start earnest thought about your mother. What kind of a child are you to this good mother of yours? No matter about your age; for whether you are younger or older, it is all the same. What kind of a child are you to your mother? We make our life beautiful only when we are true and faithful in all our relations with others. No matter to what eminence we may attain, or to what noble character, there will always be a blot on our record and on our life as God sees it, if in climbing upward ourselves we fail in any of love's duties to others. To be a complete man or woman in the world, you must be ever a loyal and faithful child to the mother to whom you owe so much.

> " God thought to give the sweetest thing
> In his almighty power
> To earth; and deeply pondering
> What it should be, one hour,
> In fondest joy and love of heart
> Outweighing every other,
> He moved the gates of heaven apart
> And gave to earth — a mother."

CHAPTER V.

ABOUT YOUR FATHER.

PERHAPS fathers have been neglected. Volumes have been written and countless sermons have been preached about mothers. Their devotion and self-sacrifice have been commented upon without stint. Children are taught to honor their mother, to remember always what she has done for them, and what they owe to her, to think of her happiness, and to care for her in her old age, with all gentleness and thoughtfulness.

This is well. No words can exaggerate the sacredness of motherhood, or the value and importance of the mother's influence on the child. God comes to us first in our mother. The old rabbis said, "God could not be everywhere, and therefore he made mothers." We cannot pay too much honor to our mother, nor do too much to bring comfort and blessing to her.

But the fathers should not be forgotten. It is not fair, for example, to do all the preaching to mothers, with scarcely a passing exhortation to fathers. Where does any one find in the Bible that mothers have all the responsibility for the training and bringing up of the children? The Scriptures certainly lay the burden upon both parents; at least, they do not put it all on the mother. The father is to teach his children the commandments of God; the mother cannot be held alone responsible for their religious instruction. It is time some sermons were prepared and preached, and some chapters written, on the solemnity and sacredness of fatherhood.

Then, in the building of the home, the father, unless he be a most unworthy man or an utter nonenity, has an essential part. There are good fathers; not all are indifferent to their home. There are many men who are truly devoted to the interests of their families. The mother may seem to get nearer a child's heart, and to be first in influence upon a child's life. But it is time an earnest word was spoken in behalf of fathers — of the nobleness and worth of their part in the home life, and the honor due to them from children.

What has your father done for you? He did not nurse you, and wash and dress you, when you were a crying baby. He did not rock your cradle, did not teach you the hundred first lessons of infancy, did not mend your playthings, help you with your dolls, nor even train you in saying your prayers. There are many things which were very important in your bringing up which most likely your father did not do. No doubt there are elements in your thoughts of your mother which have no place in your visions of fatherhood, as it forms itself before you out of memory's holy experiences.

Yet there are other elements which belong rather to fatherhood than to motherhood, and which were quite as important in the sheltering and moulding of your childhood, as those which are so idealized in the pictures of true motherhood. We think of the tenderness there is in a mother's heart, something wondrously akin to the divine tenderness, inexhaustible in its patience, its thoughtfulness, and its comforting power. But corresponding to this in the true father there is strength, strength which toils, which defends, which shelters from the rough storm, which stands like a rock. Surely strength is as divine as tenderness. There may be less sentimentality in it, but for life's practical uses its value is no less than that of the softer quality.

Think of the sturdy side of your father's character, and of what it has been to you. If your mother's love made the home-life which was like a heavenly summer to you, it was your father who built the material home in which such holy warmth was possible. It was your father who earned the money which provided the comforts. It was your father who braved the storms of winter and endured the heats of summer to make shelter for you. You never can know just how your father toiled for you, how he denied himself ofttimes that you might not want anything, how he made sacrifices that better privileges than he himself had ever enjoyed might be yours. There is something very pathetic in the way some fathers struggle and deny themselves, that they may save their children the necessity for struggle and self-denial.

Then, if you have been blessed with a good father, think of all the privileges you have enjoyed from his toil. Children are the inheritors of their father's name as well as his property. If he lives worthily, he lifts them up to a place of honor in the community. Think of the education you have had, the opportunities for growth in knowledge and wisdom. Perhaps your father had only scant schooling in his youth, and now you are in the academy or the college.

A little thought or reflection will show you

that you owe to your father a large debt for favors and blessings which are of incalculable value to you. Perhaps you have been in the habit of saying that Providence is very good to you. Yes, but your father is your providence, — under God, of course, but nevertheless indisputably; for without your father's toil and faithfulness these blessings would not have been yours. God sent them; but it was your father's hand that earned them, and gathered them about your life.

Then, apart from all this, think what your father has been to you as an influence. All through your formative years he was ever before you, coming and going, a man of truth and righteousness, diligent, punctual in his duty, brave in struggle, firm in his opinions and principles. It is no small thing to have grown up beneath the shadow of such righteousness of character. Perhaps he was stern at times, and even severe and cold, lacking the gentleness which was so beautiful in your mother; yet it was a splendid education which you got from this abiding vision of strength, truth, and justice; and you owe far more to it than you can ever understand.

Only a single glimpse of the distinguishing qualities of true fatherhood has thus been given, but it is enough to help young people to remember that they have a father as well as a mother, and that to him as well as to her they owe love, honor, and grateful treatment. Naturally, less sentiment gathers about a father in his advancing years than about a mother at like age. But no little child should ever fail of filial duty to a father. The commandment reads, "Honor *thy father* and thy mother."

The ways in which we may show honor to our father are many. We may hold his name dear and sacred. We may surround him with love — he craves gentleness and affectionateness just as much as our mother does. We may seek to be his helper in his work, interesting ourselves in it. Children are responsible for the full success of their father's life. They may tear down all that he has builded, or they may carry on to completion what he has begun, and fill his old age with joy and comfort.

But think it out for yourself, — what your father has been to you personally, what you owe to him, and how you may make fit return for what he has done for you and been to you. We may properly read the rabbi's saying thus, "God could not be everywhere, and therefore he made fathers."

CHAPTER VI.

ABOUT YOUR FRIENDS.

FRIENDSHIPS begin very early. Little children form tender associations which mean much to their happiness, and which sometimes last through their life. We all need friendships. In solitary confinement men have been known to make friends of insects and little animals, the only living creatures they could have for companions. Aloneness is one of the most pathetic experiences of human life.

Nothing is more important to young people than the choosing of their friends. Really it is almost the settling of their whole future. The kind of friends one begins with one is apt to stay with always. If you accept and choose as your friends in early youth those who are good, refined, and aspiring, you are setting your life in the direction of whatsoever things are true, just, honorable, pure, and lovely. Almost certainly your whole future will be on the same wholesome lines. But if you attach yourself then in friendship to those who are unworthy, whose life is earthly and sinful, who are not true and noble, you, in effect, fix your place and your character in a drift which will be toward things that are not good, and that do not tend to honor and beauty of soul.

There is a sense in which our friends are chosen for us before we are old enough to distinguish between the worthy and the unworthy, those who will help us upward, and those who will drag us downward. Happy is the child who is under the influence and guidance of wise and good parents, who see to it that the first friendships formed are what they should be! The indifference of parents in this matter ofttimes has been responsible for the wrecking of their children's lives. They paid no heed to the character of the playmates and companions of their earliest years; exercised no restraining influence, no discrimination, in choosing between the fit and the unfit in those whom they admitted as their children's first friends. While they slept the enemy sowed tares.

But after the years of infancy and earliest youth, young people have a great deal to do with the choosing of their own friends. I am not speaking of love between young men and young women, of love which may ripen into marriage; I am speaking of friendship, which is a different matter altogether. Love presents a "problem" of its own; but we all need common friendships, and it is very important that they be formed wisely and carefully. There is a tendency among young people to be altogether too indiscriminate in forming their friendships. All who come are admitted to a kind of general intimacy. Youth is hospitable to friendships, and is disposed to confide without question, and to make room for every new companionship that offers. There is need, however, for reserve at this point. No doubt the law of Christian love requires us to be courteous to all, even to strangers, to show the grace of kindness to every one we meet, even most casually. But we are not required to take every chance acquaintance into the place of friendship. Here we must learn to exercise the greatest caution and reserve.

Character should be made a test. Young people should shut out of their life everything that would defile or tarnish, and whatever would make it harder for them to be true and worthy. Life's battle is sore enough at best, and instead of admitting influences which would make the struggle for them more severe, they should seek always the contacts and inspirations which will make it easier for them to live nobly and worthily. To take into the life a friendship which is not good and pure, which will become a temptation toward a lower moral standard, toward a less beautiful and helpful life, toward frivolousness, indolence, irreverence, or selfishness, is, at the best, to make it harder to live beautifully. Young people should have the courage to shut out of their life all friendships whose influence could work in them only moral deterioration, and hinder their growth into the best possible character.

> " Thou shalt need all the strength that God can give
> Simply to live, my friend, simply to live."

Among other qualities, sympathy is required in those who would make us good friends. There must be intercourse, and intercourse is impossible between unsympathetic spirits. This does not necessarily mean that there shall be agreement in all their opinions — difference of view ofttimes adds interest and zest to intercourse; but the natures must have a congeniality that will make it easy for them to blend. There are natures which never can blend, — they are to each other like fire and tinder. Instead of calling out the best, each brings out the worst in the other. In deciding upon who their friends shall be, young people should choose only those with whom they can live in cordial sympathy.

It is well also that between friends the relations shall be such that neither shall be too greatly dependent on the other. One quality of all true friendship is the desire "not to be ministered unto, but to minister." A friendship whose chief object is to receive, to be helped, to be served, is only selfish. On the other hand, one must be willing to receive as well as to give. All giving and helping, with no receiving or being helped, is not a practical basis of good friendship. It is better therefore that there be, as nearly as possible, an equality of condition, so that the help given may be mutual and reciprocal.

It is not necessary that your friends should be about your own age. Every young person ought to have friends older than himself. The older are better for counsel; and the young people are fortunate indeed who have one or two wise, true, and sympathetic friends of more years than their own, to whom they can go with the serious questions and problems which continually arise in every earnest mind. Young persons often advise rashly and impetuously; an older friend, who has learned wisdom in the experiences of years, will give wiser and safer counsel.

We need to be ever seeking new friends, or at least holding our heart's doors open to receive the new friends whom God may send to us. We need new friends to take the place of those we lose as we go on our way. Death is ever busy, and no friendship is strong enough to resist his cruel hand. Friends are lost, too, in other ways, sometimes by reason of changes in life's conditions.

Then friendships seem sometimes to be outgrown. We deplore their dying out, when perhaps the truth is that these friendships were sent to us on a definite errand, to minister to us in a particular way and but for a time. Then, when their ministry is completed, they fall off. But we have not really lost them, nor should we ever forget them, or the part they have had in the making of our life. God sends us new friends for new needs, not to displace the old, but to carry on the good which the old began. Robert Louis Stevenson tells us that, —

"The dearest friends are the auldest friends,
And the young are just on trial."

One friend is not enough. Some young people are inclined to make one very intimate friendship, and to allow that to exclude all other companionships. Sometimes they are so exacting as to demand that the one favored friend shall scarcely even treat any other person kindly. Such an exacting spirit is very narrow, showing utter selfishness and want of confidence in the friend who is held in such bondage.

Young people will do well, also, to guard against too great and too unreserved intimacy even with their best friends. There is sure to be an estrangement sooner or later if the association is too close or free. For example, when two girls are seen always together, almost giving up every other friendship and companionship for each other, it is usually safe to predict a short-lived intimacy. By and by they grow tired of each other. It is better always, even in the closest friendship, to maintain a measure of reserve, never to give all, not to see too much of each other. A friendship which exercises wise self-restraint, which is not too emotional, too free and unreserved, will prove the surest and the most lasting, and in all ways the most wholesome.

It need not even be said that young people would better chose for their friends those who love and follow Christ. There is a wondrous secret of safety in Christian companionship. The intercourse which deepens into true Christian fellowship is very sacred. The friendship which is hallowed by the love of Christ is woven of a threefold cord which cannot be broken. God reveals his love to us in the love of our true Christian friends. It is he who gives us our friends, and we must recognize the gift with reverence and love.

It is well for us to remember that friendship requires also something on our part. It cannot be all on one side. Love may be, but friendship must give as well as receive. It costs to be a friend. Then we must be worthy if we would take another life into the place of confidence and affection. Charles Lamb warned a young man who was disposed to confide in him that he was not good enough to be his friend. We need to make sure that our heart is pure and that our hands are clean before we accept the confidence and trust of a human heart. Then we must be loyal and faithful to our friend, once chosen, whatever the cost may be.

CHAPTER VII.

BEGINNING A CHRISTIAN LIFE.

EVERY young person should be a Christian. All the heart's truest instincts would lead the soul to God. Christ alone can answer our cravings and satisfy our longings. In him alone can any one find himself, and reach the things that are true and right and lovely.

How may one begin to be a Christian? The hunger is in the heart, the desire to take Christ as Saviour and Master; but many a young person passes through a long experience of painful anxiety and perplexity in finding the way into the light of faith and peace. A friend, knowing that I am considering young people's problems, writes in a personal letter: " Some time will you ask people to help children to come to Christ and confess him? Oh, the weeks and months that I suffered, trying to gain courage to speak to my mother before she guessed it and came to me!"

This is a common experience of childhood. Children long to have some one to speak to them about Christ, so that they can voice their heart's yearnings, and come out in joyful acceptance and confession of Christ. They love Christ, and want to speak of their love; but they need the touch of human love to help them. Happy are the young people who at this critical point in their spiritual history have wise, gentle, patient guidance.

To begin to be a Christian is to learn that God loves you; that you are his child; that Jesus Christ stands beside you, asking you to believe in him, to commit your life to him; and that you may without fear, doubt, or reserve, trust him. It is not by our love for Christ that we are saved, but by Christ's love for us. Faith in Christ is simply the acceptance of divine friendship. You need not trouble yourself about the smallness of your love or the feebleness of your faith; your hope and your security are not measured either by your love or by your faith, but by the infinite love and strength in which you are trusting.

The first thing is to get your relation with Christ clearly established. He loves you, and you accept his love. He would take your life as it is, with all its sin, fault, and shortcoming, as you put it into his hands. You need not understand it all, — there is no reason why you should. You believe that Christ has all power, all wisdom, all love. His hands are safe hands, skilful hands, gentle hands, hands of love. He can take your soul, which sin has hurt and stained, no matter how sorely, and restore it to beauty. Faith is the committing of the life to him for salvation, for guidance, for care and keeping, for time and eternity.

Then the next step is the acceptance of Christ as your Master and Lord. A Christian is one who follows Christ. This means the surrender of the whole life to him. The heart must be given up. There can be no Christian life without love. Jesus demands the first place in the affections of his followers. If any one loves father or mother, brother or sister, wife or child, more than him, he is not worthy of him, and cannot be his disciple.

Soldiers may obey implicitly without love; but the most perfect obedience, if the heart be not in it, would not make one a Christian. We might devote our life and strength to Christian work, toiling unweariedly in the service of the church, giving our money lavishly for the advancement of Christianity or for the relief of suffering, and yet not be Christians. Love for Christ must be the motive at the heart of all our work. "Lovest thou me?" is the test.

But the heart draws the whole life after it. If we love, we will serve. "If ye love me, keep my commandments." "Ye are my friends, if ye do whatsoever I command you." We cannot accept Christ as our Saviour, and not at the same time accept him as our Master. We must begin at once to obey him; and our obedience must be without reserve, without condition, without question. It must also be cheerful and glad-hearted, not compulsory, reluctant, or constrained. Christians are soldiers of Christ, and the soldier's first duty is to obey. Whether the will of Christ be made known to us in his word, through our own conscience, or in providence, we should always promptly and cheerfully accept and obey. It may not be always easy — it may be very hard and costly; but when the will of our Master is made known, if we are his followers we can only obey, and our obedience should be sweet with love.

Consecration is nothing but being a Christian from the centre of our heart to the tips of our fingers, and being a Christian always, wherever we go. "Whose I am and whom I serve" was one great Christian's idea of the life we should live. A Christian belongs to Christ, and knows it and remembers it wherever he is.

Jesus spoke Mary's name — she did not recognize him before, she supposed him to be the gardener; but when he said " Mary!" she knew him, and from her heart said, " Rabboni!" It is always just that way. We love him because he first loved us; we know him because he first calls us. He speaks our name, and then we say "Rabboni, Master!" Christ is ours and we are Christ's. That is becoming a Christian. Then, being a Christian is living out that same life of love, obedience, surrender, and service, through all the days.

There is something else; he who loves Christ loves his brother also. To begin to be a Christian is to remove from the arctic zone of cold selfishness into the warm summer zone of love. We cannot make too much of our relation to Christ, — that is the beginning of it all; but we have relations to others as well. We are to live in the thirteenth chapter of First Corinthians, with love that suffereth long and is kind, that envieth not, is not puffed up, doth not behave itself unseemly, seeketh not its own, is not provoked, beareth all things, endureth all things. The Christian life that does not make us more gentle, more patient, more unselfish, is not realizing its true meaning. A Christian life is a new Christ-life lived out in this world — we are to be Christ to others.

When we love Christ we will want our brother to love him too. We will strive to bring others to him to find the same joy we have found. We will seek to bring back the one who is wandering. One writes the lesson thus : —

> " First seek thy Saviour out, and dwell
>   Beneath the shadow of his roof,
> Till thou have scanned his features well,
>   And known him for the Christ by proof, —
>
> Such proof as they are sure to find,
>   Who spend with him their happy days;
> Clean hands and a self-ruling mind,
>   Ever in tune for love and praise.
>
> Then, potent with the spell of heaven,
>   Go, and thine erring brother gain;
> Entice him home to be forgiven,
>   Till he, too, sees his Saviour plain."

The heart of the Christian should be a well of living water, a fount of holy and blessed influences, whose streams flow in all directions, carrying comfort, cheer, encouragement, help, and gladness to every other life they reach. Mere orthodoxy of belief does not make one a Christian, nor does attention to ecclesiastical rites and rules; a Christian is one in whom the life of Christ pulses and the love of Christ glows and burns.

When should a young person become a Christian? At once, is the answer — to-day. Not an hour should be lost. The whole life belongs to Christ, not the mature years alone, but the earliest days as well; not the ripe fruit merely, but the bud and the flower as well; not the mid-day only, with its heat and burden, but the morning, too, with its sweetness and freshness. One cannot come too early to Christ. Listen to the first gentle voices in your heart. Yield to the first influences of the divine Spirit. Give Christ the beginnings of your life.

It is a serious mistake for young people to wait until they can begin with deep experiences and conspicuous activities; they should begin as little children. Christian life is a school; we are to enter the lowest forms and become learners, advancing day by day. "Come unto me, and learn of me," is the Master's invitation. The best time to begin a Christian life is in childhood, when the heart is tender, when it is easy to learn.

> "He who waits to have his task marked out
> Shall die and leave his errand unfulfilled."

CHAPTER VIII.

GETTING ACQUAINTED WITH CHRIST.

Many young Christians do not get to know Christ as a personal friend for a good while after they have begun trusting him as their Saviour. This is natural; for we cannot see Christ, nor hear his voice, and it is only through experience that we can get acquainted with him as a friend. Yet it may help some young Christians to think a little of this subject.

Late one night I was sent for to visit a young woman who was in the last stages of consumption. She belonged to a household of orphaned children. From her infancy she had faithfully maintained the habit of daily prayer. She had read her Bible, attended church services, and had lived a good life, quiet, thoughtful, beautiful, without blame. There is no doubt that she had been a Christian for years.

Yet when I sat at her bedside that night, and began to speak with her, I saw that she had no conscious personal friendship with Christ. I spoke to her, gently as I could, of God's wonderful love for her. I told her that God was her Father, and that he had been caring for her with infinite tenderness all her years. I then spoke to her of Jesus Christ, of his dying for her, and then of his being alive. I dwelt especially upon the fact that he had been her companion, her guide, her protector, her personal friend, all through her life.

When I had spoken thus for a little while, she looked up into my face and said, with an expression I cannot soon forget, "And I never knew him!" It was a moment of revelation to her. For the first time in all her life she was becoming conscious of the personal relation of Christ to her. She now became aware, as by the sudden lifting of a veil, of One standing by her side, One who had been with her all her life, who had been blessing her in countless gentle ways, who had ministered to her from the riches of his love and grace, but whom, until this moment, she had never recognized.

From that time until she was lifted away into the heavenly life, she lived in sweet, conscious enjoyment of Christ's presence, companionship, and love. All that was wanted was to make her aware of the presence and companionship of the Friend in whom she had been trusting. She had long been receiving the blessings of divine grace, but now for the first time she had a glimpse of him from whom the blessings had come.

No doubt there are many young Christians who are living just as this young woman had lived — receiving into their heart the comforts of Christ's grace without fully enjoying the blessings of personal friendship with him. They know Christ as a historical personage, being familiar with the facts of his story as told in the Gospels. They trust him as their Saviour. They accept the mercy which comes through his sacrifice, having in their heart the peace of forgiveness. They rest on his promises, and draw grace from his fulness. But they do not know the living, personal Christ. Not only is he to them unseen; he is also unrecognized.

No one can estimate the measure of comfort and blessedness which one misses who remains thus unaware of the presence and companionship of the living Christ. He misses all that personal friendship with Christ means, and no words can describe the richness and power of this friendship.

Indeed, many Christians seem never to get any farther than the cross in their knowledge of Christ. They believe that he loved them and gave himself for them. They believe that their hope of salvation comes from the atonement. They believe the historical fact of the resurrection, when Christ conquered death. They speak of him as now in heaven making intercession for them. They get a measure of comfort for the future, for themselves and for their loved ones who die in Christian faith, from the fact of Christ's victory over death. But they miss the meaning of his promise, "Lo, I am with you all the days."

Really, however, we are saved, not alone by the death of Christ for us, but by Christ himself with us and in us. It is into fellowship with the living Redeemer that faith brings us. It is believing in a person that saves us. Christ and we become friends. We walk together. He shares all our toil, care, burden-bearing, struggle, weakness, and sorrow, imparting to us his grace, strength, help, and all the inspirations of his love. "Henceforth I call you — friends," is his own word.

We may go still farther; for not only is Christ *with* us — he is also *in* us. One of the striking words of St. Paul in his Epistle to the Galatians is, "It pleased God . . . to reveal his Son in me." There is a difference between revealing the Son to a man as a friend standing beside him, and revealing the Son in a man, dwelling in his own heart, possessing, absorbing, and inspiring his very life.

Rev. F. B. Meyer in one of his sermons quotes this word of St. Paul's, and then says that many Christians fail to get this revelation of Jesus Christ in them, and that many do not for years after conversion come to this experience. He gives this illustration: A boy left his home and was gone a great while, nothing ever being heard from him. His widowed mother, in her struggles with sorrow and poverty, never ceased to pray for her boy; but years and years passed and he came not again. One day there was a knock at the door; and, when the woman answered it, a young man stood there. She did not know him. He asked if he could get lodging in her house. She said she had a room that she could give him. Then he asked if he could have boarding with her. To this also she replied affirmatively. He remained with her for several weeks, coming and going. One day, at the table, some turn of his hand showed to the mother a mark which at once revealed her own boy to her. "O Tom!" she exclaimed, with loving eagerness. "It's my own boy." God revealed her son to her, in her home.

So it is that Christ lives in the heart of many

believers for years and years, inspiring in them good and beautiful things, blessing their life, granting them favors and mercies, yet all the time unrecognized by them. Then at length there comes to them an experience of revealing. It may be in time of sorrow, or in the shadows of a sick-room; or it may be in a sweet human friendship, or in a sermon, or in a verse of Scripture. In some way at least God reveals his Son to them; and in the midst of the love that flows about them they see the face of the Beloved, from whom for so long they have been receiving blessings, but whom till this moment they have not known.

It is the privilege of every Christian to have Christ, not only as a friend, walking by his side in close and daily companionship, but also living in his heart, with all the warmth and inspiration of divine love and grace. We miss infinite comfort and joy by not recognizing this unseen Friend. There would seem to be no reason why any one should fail to recognize him. The promise is plain and sure that every one who believes has not only the constant companionship of Christ, but also Christ living in him.

Young Christians will find a wondrous new blessing in getting personally acquainted with

Christ, and in taking him as their intimate, confidential Friend. It will change all life for them to have the assurance and the consciousness of this blessed friendship. It will make all burdens lighter, and all tasks easier, and sorrow less bitter. It will put a new meaning into all duty. It will fill the heart full of joy. Yet that is what it is to be a Christian, — having Christ for our Friend. No other friend should be so near and so real to us as Jesus Christ.

CHAPTER IX.

ABOUT CONSECRATION.

No word is more frequently used by young people in these days than the word consecration. Indeed, it is used so frequently, and falls from the lips so glibly, that there is danger of its true meaning not being always appreciated. Precisely what do young Christians mean — or older ones — when they talk about consecration? What effect has their act of consecration upon their life?

Consecration is personal devotement to God. By this act we profess to set ourselves apart for God and for God's service. We confess that we belong to Christ because he has bought us with a price; and we say that we recognize his ownership, and lay ourselves upon the altar for his use. If our act be sincere, we will regard all our life as belonging to him. Our hands are his, to be used in doing his work; and they must be kept clean for him, and do only worthy things. Our lips are his, to speak only for him, and words only that will please him. Our heart is his, to cherish only the affections, feelings, and motives which are consistent with his Spirit and his will. Our feet are his, to walk with God, and to run on his errands. Our money is his, to be used by us for him. Our whole life is his; we are not our own, and we are to live for the honoring and glorifying of Christ's name.

But precisely what does all this mean? The difficulty lies in bringing down this lofty ideal consecration from its spiritual and ethereal heights, and interpreting it into the common life of our common days. We do not live among the stars; we live yet on the earth. We have to do with earthly things. The greater portion of our time is taken up with what we call secular work and duties. We must live in human relations, in our home, in society, mingling with people in business, in school, in amusements. How shall we carry out the principles of our consecration in this earthly life?

For one thing, we must live out the teachings of Christ in all that we do, in our daily life in the world, as well as in our relations with God. If young people are at school, they must be diligent in their studies, and kindly and unselfish in all their relations with schoolmates and teachers. That is, they must be Christians at school. In home life they must manifest, in all their relations with the members of their household, the affections and dispositions which are inspired by Christ. They must be thoughtful, kindly, patient, unselfish, not easily provoked, thinking no evil, ready in all ways and at all times to serve. If they are employed in any business or calling, they must do the duties which are assigned to them with faithfulness and with alacrity, never taking advantage of kindness to shirk work, always honest and truthful, always patient and courteous. In their social relations they must maintain the principles of Christianity, never forgetting, when they meet worldly or wicked people, that they belong to Christ, and are to be worthy of him.

This does not mean that they should be talking all the time about religion — there is a time to speak out boldly for Christ, and there is a time when silence, even concerning religious matters, is better than speech. But it means that they are never to do anything inconsistent with the Christian life, anything that would bring reproach upon the name of Christ.

A little girl, applying for membership in a church, when asked by the pastor what she thought it would be for her to be a Christian, replied: "I suppose it will be to do what Jesus would do, and to behave as Jesus would behave, if he were a little girl and lived at our house." There could be no better definition of a consecrated life. We are always to ask, "What would Jesus do?" and then try to do the same. A Christian is always a Christian, wherever he may go. He is never off duty. He always represents Christ. He must always strive to be what Jesus would be, and to do what Jesus would do in his place.

One of the most common weaknesses of much of our consecration is the effort to grasp the thought in too large a way, to make the consecration once for all, rather than in detail. For example, each morning, as we begin the day, we may give ourselves to our Master just for the one little day. We may ask him to take us and keep us and use us.

We then take up our allotment of tasks for the day, feeling that it is Christ's work we are doing, and therefore that it is holy. It is just as much a part of our Christian duty to learn a lesson in school, to sell goods in the store, to perform a duty in the office, to plough in the field, to sweep a room, or to cook a meal, as it was in the early morning to go apart for prayer and Bible-reading. We are to regard all the tasks and duties of the day as holy, and as part of our consecrated life.

If, then, in the providence of God, there break into our plan for the day interruptions, — human needs, for example, which require sympathy, thought, time, or money, — we are to regard these as fragments of service sent to us from God. They are bits of God's will breaking into our human plan; and we are to regard them as sacred, and do them cheerfully, even if they take our time and cost us trouble.

Living thus, holding our whole life to be used by the Master as he would use it, diligent in our business, losing no moment of time, we are to fill our day with tasks and duties well and faithfully done. This is consecration. No other kind of living is worthy of the name. We cannot be always at prayer, or always reading our Bible; and it is a mistake to think that consecration has to do only with these spiritual acts and exercises. It has to do quite as much with the secularities of life, although, indeed, this spirit makes all our duties holy.

Even our amusements and our pleasures are to be considered part of our life of consecration. Therefore, nothing must be entered into which would dishonor Christ. We should go to no place which we would not be willing to have

Christ see us entering. We should engage in nothing which would make us ashamed if his face were to appear in the doorway.

There is a too common impression that nothing is religious save what is essentially religious in its form. Thus many people fail to carry their consecration outside the church and the prayer-meeting. They are very devout in their feeling and manner while a service lasts, but fail to live devoutly when the service is over, and they are mingling again with their fellows. We should remember that consecration is not a matter of feeling, but of disposition, of conduct, of character, of words and deeds. If, therefore, it is something only for a holy place, or for a sacred service, which fades from our face and life when we go out, it is not genuine. Consecration is not a frame; it is a life.

It is never encouraging to see people put on an unusual solemnity of manner in an effort to be consecrated Christians. There are some good young men and women who seem to think that consecration should make them grave and serious. They talk in solemn, unnatural tones. They are oppressed with a kind of spiritual self-consciousness which makes them anything but lovely or lovable Christians in the eyes of other people. They may be thoroughly sincere; but their assumption of sanctity, as it appears in their bearing, makes them very imperfect representatives of Christ. It even leads some persons to suspect the genuineness of their religion.

Thus, instead of honoring Christ by a goodness which is beautiful as well as true, they hurt their influence as Christians. Religion should be natural; anything that is unnatural is in so far un-Christlike. "Whatsoever things are lovely" is one of St. Paul's phrases describing the ideal Christian life. Sanctimoniousness is very unlovely. Persons who put on holy airs, fancying that thus they are proving themselves consecrated, are only showing their religious self-conceit. Simplicity is a mark of all beautiful Christian life. Moses was not aware of the shining of his face. The truest, divinest goodness is never conscious of itself.

True consecration does not require that a child's religion shall be that of the full-grown man or woman. One of the dangers of a young Christian's life is in this direction. He is apt to take his ideal from older Christians, and to imitate them. We know what happens if we try to open a rosebud and hasten its unfolding; we only spoil the bud, and hinder it from ever becoming a lovely rose. It is the same when a young Christian tries to be a grown-up Christian. The charm of the young Christian character is spoiled, and the life is so hurt that it will never be what it might have been if it had been left to develop naturally.

Consecration in young Christians, therefore, means the beautifying, enriching, and sanctifying of their youth. Jesus himself waited thirty years in quiet before he entered upon his public ministry. His consecration led him to obey his parents, to help in the carpenter shop, and to do the common duties that came to his hands. There can be no higher example for any young Christians. They are to do the duties that belong to their age, thus preparing themselves for the more serious responsibilities and tasks of maturer years.

CHAPTER X.

ABOUT PRAYER.

ALMOST every one prays. At least almost every one is taught in childhood to kneel before God, and with the first lispings of speech to say, "Our Father." And all Christians maintain the habit of prayer with more or less faithfulness.

What is prayer? It is not merely making requests of God. This is part of it; we are to make known our requests to him. We are to bring to him all our needs, small and large; and we are assured that, while nothing is too great to lay upon God, nothing is too small to trouble him with. The God who cares for the birds, feeds the quarrelsome sparrows, and clothes the lilies of the field, cares much more for his children, supplying their wants. In our prayers we are to make requests to God for the things we need.

But prayer is more than this. It includes confession of sins. We all sin against God, and we need every day to ask him for forgiveness.

Then part of all true prayer is thanksgiving — remembering our blessings, other answered prayers. Prayer includes also communion with God. Our relation to him is that of a child to a father. Surely that child would be wanting in filial affection who would never care to talk to a father, save when it had some request to make of him, some favor to ask. A large part of loving intercourse between child and father is fellowship, conversation about things in which both are interested. So the Christian who cares to pray only when he has some request to make is lacking in the truly filial spirit.

> "It is not prayer,
> This clamor of our eager wants
> That fills the air
> With wearying, selfish plaints.
>
> It is true prayer,
> To seek the Giver more than gifts;
> God's life to share
> And love — for this our cry to lift."

Many times, when we come to God in prayer, we have no favor to ask, but merely desire to be with him, to commune with him, to keep ourselves in his love, to tell him of our love, to talk to him of our plans, and to receive into our heart the blessings which he has to give.

Are prayers answered? Does God in heaven hear his children when they kneel on earth and speak to him? The Bible assures us that God is the hearer and the answerer of prayer. This does not mean that everything we ask for in prayer is given to us. Ofttimes the things we desire would not be the best things for us. Our judgment is imperfect, our vision is short-sighted, and we cannot tell whether the things we wish for would be good for us or not. All true praying requires the final submission of every request to the will and the wisdom of God. We are to trust him more than we trust ourselves. If he sees fit to deny us the things we ask, we should be sure that his way is better than ours.

It is very important that young people get into their heart, at the beginning of their Christian life, this confidence in God. Many persons have lost their faith because their prayers have not been answered. They had misread the promises, supposing that anything they would ask would be given to them. They then made requests which were not granted. In their disappointment they lost their faith, and passed into the darkness of doubt and unbelief. If we understand that every desire we bring we are to submit to God's wisdom, however intense it may be, abiding by his decision without murmuring, without fear, we shall never find ourselves in perplexity because of what seems to us to be God's failure to answer our prayers.

> "I sometimes think God's tender heart must ache,
> Listening to all the sad, complaining cries
> That from our weak, impatient souls arise,
> Because we do not see that for our sake
> He answers not, or answers otherwise
> Than seems the best to our tear-blinded eyes."

When God does not give us the things we definitely ask for, it is because he desires to give us something better instead. St. Paul asked for the removal of his "thorn in the flesh," some sore bodily trouble. He asked earnestly, three times beseeching the Lord to grant his request. The request was not granted; but instead there came the promise of sufficient grace — more grace because of the burden of pain and suffering which he was still to keep. Then he rejoiced in his infirmities, because through them he received more of the strength of Christ. Jesus himself, in the garden, prayed that the cup might pass from him. It did not pass; but instead, divine grace was given, and he was enabled to accept it without murmuring. His prayer was answered, not by the removal of the cup, but by the strengthening of his own heart, so that he could drink it with quiet submission.

The lesson is very clear. When God does not give us the things we plead for, he will give us grace to do without them, and if we accept his decision sweetly and trustingly, will enable us to go on rejoicing. Surely it is a better answer to give us strength to continue bearing our load than it would have been to take it away, leaving us unstrengthened.

What may we bring to God in prayer? We ought to bring everything, not only our spiritual needs, and our sorrows and perplexities, but our business affairs, our friendships, our frets and worries — all our life. Christ wants us to be his close personal friends. He desires to enter into the most intimate relations with each of us. He wants our confidence at every point. He is interested in everything we do — in our daily work, in our plans and efforts, in the children's play, in the young people's problems, pleasures, and studies. We should train ourselves to talk to Christ of everything we are doing. Anything we do not want to talk to him about we would better not do. It is a sad day for a boy when he has done something which he wants to hide from his mother. It is a sad day for any of us when we have done anything we are not willing to talk to Christ about. We would better ask his counsel concerning everything we are considering. Coleridge well exhorts:—

> If for any wish thou darest not pray,
> Then pray to God to cast that wish away.

When should we pray? Part of the pledge which young people all over the world are making these days is that they will pray every day. We should pray at least twice every day. We should begin the morning at Christ's feet, seeking blessing from him, asking for guidance, putting our hand in his, intrusting our life to his keeping. Then when we come to the close of the day, there should be prayer again, the bringing of the day's work to God, the confessing of its faults, sins, and mistakes, the laying at our Master's feet of all the work we have done, and the committing of ourselves to his keeping for the night.

But besides these formal seasons of prayer, morning and evening, every Christian should be always in the spirit of prayer. We walk with God in our every-day life. Christ is just as close to us when we are at our daily work in the field, in the shop, in the store, or when we are sitting at our desk in school, or are out on the playground, as he is when we are kneeling at his feet in a formal act of prayer. Anywhere and at any time we may whisper a request, or speak a word of love in his ear, and he will hear us.

That is what St. Paul means by his exhortation that we be "instant in prayer." He would have us stay all the time so close to Christ that any moment a word may be exchanged with him — that we may speak to him or he to us. In time of temptation, when the pressure is sore, almost more than we are able to endure, it is a great privilege to say, "Jesus, help me." In some moment of perplexity as to duty, we may ask our Guide to show us what he would have us to do, and he will do it. If we are in danger we may run into the refuge of prayer, hiding ourselves close to Christ, as a frightened bird flies to its nest, or as an alarmed child runs to the mother.

Those who learn to pray in this way, communing with Christ continually, are sure of rich blessing in their life. Prayer makes us stronger. It brings the divine life down into our heart. It shelters us amid temptation. It keeps us near the heart of Christ in time of sorrow or danger.

It transforms us into the beauty of the Master. Prayer brings heaven down close about us, into our heart. Prayer keeps us close to Christ; one who prays daily, and continues instant in prayer, will never drift far from him. It is when we begin to omit prayer that we begin to leave Christ.

In these wise modern days many sceptical questions are asked concerning prayer, but a simple faith answers them all. If God is our Father, he surely knows his children and loves them. If this be true, there can be no doubt that he is interested in their life in this world, and is willing to communicate with them — to speak to them, and to hear them when they speak to him. There need, then, be no mystery about prayer; it is only one of the privileges of the children of God.

CHAPTER XI.

THE BIBLE IN THE CLOSET.

We are continually reminded of the necessity for secret prayer. We are taught that we should both begin and end each busy day at the Master's feet. This is all very well. Not a word too much can be said on the importance of prayer. We cannot live a spiritual life at all unless we draw the inspiration down from heaven. In our life in this world of evil and struggle, we are like divers working on board a sunken ship beneath the waves of the sea; we can maintain our life and continue our work only by keeping unbroken communication with heaven, and by breathing heaven's air.

But it is a mistake to suppose that prayer alone is sufficient to nourish our spiritual life. It is just as needful to have God talk to us as it is for us to talk to him. Yet we are not exhorted in books and sermons half so frequently or half so earnestly to read our Bible, as part of our daily spiritual feeding, as we are to pray.

There are many people who rarely carry the Bible with them into their closet. They drop on their knees for a few hurried moments in the morning, and implore God's blessing on them for the day; and then they are up and away, carrying no word of God in their heart as they enter the day's strifes and toils. Really they have had only half a meal, and are not prepared as they might have been for duty. They should have eaten some of the words of God, and then they would have been truly invigorated and made strong for their day's pilgrimage.

In all ordinary cases God gives spiritual help through his word. He does not now talk to men as he talked to Moses on the mount; if we would hear what he has to say to us, we must open his word, and read its pages for ourselves with listening ear. He really has something to say to us every time we enter our closet. Perhaps the day is dark before us, and we are going out not knowing which way to turn. We cry for light. What lamp will God put into our hands, unless it be a precept or a promise? Yet we shall not carry any light with us out of our closet if we only pray, and do not open our Bible. The old psalm-writer did not say, "Prayer is a lamp unto my feet, and a light unto my path." It is the word of God which is to shed this brightening on our way.

Or we may be in sorrow, and in our quest for consolation we turn away from unsatisfying human words and empty earthly comforts to the closet of prayer. We ask God to comfort us. Now it is very sweet sometimes, when the sorrow is bitter and the darkness intense, just to lay our head on our Master's bosom in silence, saying nothing at all, not even praying in words. There is comfort in simply resting within the embrace of the everlasting arms. But, if we would get real, positive comfort from God, it must come from his word. To leave the Bible closed while we cry to heaven for comforting, is really to shut our ears to the angel of consolation whom we have asked God to send to us.

In all phases of experience the same is true. Prayer alone does not fit us for living sweetly and victoriously. We need the words of God, that we may use them along our way. We have an illustration of this in our Lord's own experience. When he was tempted of the devil, he answered every assault of the adversary with a word of Scripture. He did not rely on prayer alone, but in each case drew out an arrow from his well-filled quiver, and shot it at the enemy. It will be noticed, too, that he did not take out his Bible then and there, on the field, and look up a text to suit his need; he was so familiar with the words of his Father that he had but to recall from memory the particular one he required that moment. This shows us that Jesus had been in the habit of using the Bible in his closet all his early years. In the sudden temptations which come to each of us every day, we need the same equipment. We should carry with us always a quiver full of arrows from which we may draw at an instant's notice. If our closet devotion consists of prayer only, we shall find ourselves defenceless many a time in the place of danger.

There is another phase of Christian life in which the same necessity is apparent. A great artist, when asked how he could paint such marvellous pictures, replied, "I dream dreams, and I see visions; and then I paint my dreams and my visions." In our seasons of retirement with Christ we should catch glimpses of heavenly beauty, which we may then work out in act and character as we live among our fellows; we should dream dreams and see visions in the closet, which we may paint on the canvas of actual life, that others may behold them. It is only in the words of God that we can see these visions of heavenly beauty.

These inspired words show us God's thoughts and God's will, what he wants us to do, what we are to be in the life that is complete and full. We need, then, to look at these divine words in our silent times, to ponder them till they open and disclose the fragment of beauty that is in them; and then we can come out and reproduce the beauty in our own life. If we study the Scriptures when alone with God in the holy mount, God will show us in them the patterns of character, disposition, and duty, which he wants us to work out for his glory in our daily common life. The Bible shows us what we ought to be and to do; prayer brings down grace and strength to enable us to be obedient to these heavenly visions.

So we need always to take the Bible with us into the closet. Prayer alone is but half of true soul-feeding.

CHAPTER XII.

THE MATTER OF CONVERSATION.

Most young people can talk. They begin it quite early. One of the first things a baby does is to learn a language, meanwhile acquiring the use of its vocal organs. From that time, until the voice is silenced in death, the talking goes on. Some people even talk in their sleep, so strong is the force of habit upon them.

If every word that is spoken were only a good word, what an incalculable ministry of blessing would there be in a lifetime of speech! But too much of it is only idle words, and too much of it is not pure, good, and sweet. The subject is worthy of very earnest, serious thought. We should not be willing to misuse our gift of speech, or to fail to use it to bless the world.

> "Plant blessings, and blessings will bloom,
>   Plant hate, and hate will grow;
> You can sow to-day, and to-morrow shall bring
> The bloom that shows what sort of a thing
>   Is the seed—the seed that you sow."

There should be great care taken, first of all, with the manner of speech. Many persons speak most important words, words full of wisdom, and yet utter them in such a way that they make almost no impression. Their voice is harsh and unmusical, or their grammar or pronunciation is defective, or they speak indistinctly. In some way, at least, the faultiness or ungracefulness of their speech mars, sometimes almost destroys, the value of what they say. On the other hand, there are some persons whose manner of speech is so graceful and winning that even their most commonplace words fall like music on the listener's ear. Young people cannot give too much attention to voice-culture, and to the whole matter of expression. Manner is more than one-half in speech.

Matter is also important, however. We must have something to say, or the most musical tones will soon fail to please and bless. Jesus said that out of the abundance of the heart the mouth speaketh. Hence we must get our heart right if we would speak words that are worth while. A bitter heart cannot give out sweet words, nor an impure heart bright, clean words.

It is an interesting fact that on the Day of

Pentecost the Holy Spirit came in the form of tongues of fire, resting on the heads of the disciples, and that one of the first manifestations of the Spirit was in a new gift of speech — immediately they spoke with new tongues. This was all supernatural; but it is true evermore that, when one becomes a Christian, one gets a new tongue.

We can gather from the Bible many counsels about speech. Jesus spoke of idle words, saying that even for these we must give account. Idle words are those that are empty — empty of love and of good, words of no value. There are many such words spoken. They may appear harmless; and yet they are useless, and uselessness always disappoints the Master. They give no comfort, they put no cheer into any heart, they inspire nothing beautiful in any soul. Too much of the common conversation of the parlor, of the wayside, of the table, is of this vapid and empty order, — talk about merest nothings, inane, without thought, without sense, without meaning. How it must astonish the angels to hear immortal beings use their marvellous gift of speech in such a trivial, idle way!

We have suggestions also in the New Testament as to the kind of speech that is worthy of a redeemed life. St. Paul has some very plain words on the subject. Conversation should be "good, to the use of edifying." That is, no word should be spoken which does not help to build up character and to make those who hear it better, which does not inspire some good thought, some holy feeling, some kindly act, or put some touch of beauty upon the life. A Christian's words should also "minister grace unto the hearer." That is, they should impart blessing in some way. We all know persons whose words have this quality. They are not always exhorting, preaching, talking religiously; and yet we never speak with them five minutes without being the better for it. Their simplest words do us good. They give cheer, courage, and hope. We feel braver and stronger after a little conversation with them, even after a moment's greeting on the street.

In another place St. Paul says, "Let your speech be always with grace, seasoned with salt." This means graceful speech, not merely as to its manner, but also as to its quality. It must be speech such as Christ himself would use if he were in our place, and we know that every word of his was a holy seed. Our speech should be seasoned with salt, that is, should be pure and clean. Salt preserves from decay and putridity. The Christian's speech should have in it the divine quality of holiness, and its effect should be cleansing and purifying. Some one speaks of the words of Jesus himself as a handful of spices cast into this world's bitter waters to sweeten them. Every Christian's words should have like influence in society, wherever they are spoken.

This does not imply that all a Christian's words must be devout words, such as would be spoken in a prayer-meeting or in a church service. Sometimes they may be full of humor; fun may be as religious in its place as prayer in its place. There is a time to laugh and to make others laugh. We must not suppose that all bright, merry words are wrong, that we are not pleasing our Master unless we are talking on some distinctively religious subject; we are to talk of many things that are not definitely connected with a religious life. We are to talk about business, about the happenings of the day, about the books we have been reading; at proper times we are to talk of things that amuse. Ofttimes the divinest service we can render to another is to make him laugh.

Yet all the while our speech is to be with grace; it is to be true, reverent, helpful, inspiring. The seasoning is important; it is to be "seasoned with salt." Love is salt. Truth is salt. Our speech should be always kindly. It should be without bitterness, without malice, without unlovingness in any form. The seasoning should be salt; some people use pepper instead, and pepper is sharp, biting, pungent. Their speech is full of sarcasm, of censure, of bitterness, of words that hurt and burn. This is not Christlike speech.

We learn most of our lessons at home. The household life leaves its stamp on the character and the habits of each member of the family. We learn to talk at home. Defects of speech, mispronunciations, misuse of words, peculiarities of phrase, modes of expression, and all the vocal mannerisms of the common home conversation, reappear in the speech of the members of the family.

It is very important, therefore, that in the daily life of the household the most careful watch shall be kept over all the habits of speech. The tones of the voice should be cultivated so that they shall be always pleasing. Attention should be given to pronunciation, that it shall always be correct. A good dictionary is important in every house. The spirit of the conversation should be guarded, that it be gentle, kindly, patient, and true. Bickering, strife, contention, and wrangling should have no place in the talk of the home.

In too many families the household life is marred by harsh words, which are spoken too freely in the common intercourse. Sometimes it is a habit of contradicting and disputing, which has been allowed to grow until it has become inveterate. Usually the questions wrangled over are of no importance whatever. One says it was two o'clock, and another says it was a quarter past two; and they grow hot in contention over it. One says it was Wednesday, another claims that it was Thursday; and the miserable strife spoils a meal for all that family. Some young people will never answer a question asked at home, but in a gruff, discourteous way, as if the asking for information were an impertinence. There are families in which gentle and kindly speech is the exception; the staple talk is ill-tempered, dictatorial, or unloving.

There is a great deal of hasty speech in some homes. We hurt most our dearest ones by our hot words. Outside we dare not speak petulantly and angrily, for our neighbors would resent such language; but in the inner circle of love we remove the restraint, and our words too often cut deep into tender hearts. We should remember that, though love forgives hasty speech, the wounds remain. We should always hold back the word of anger.

Such home habits in conversation do not prepare one for genial and helpful intercourse with others when one goes out into the world. The loved ones of our own family are very patient with us in our unlovableness; but other people will not brook our rude manners, our discourteous retorts, our gruff talk. If the young people would be ready for living in friendly relations with those they meet outside, they must learn to control their speech in the freedom of their own home, and must train themselves there into whatsoever things are lovely both in manner and matter of conversation.

Too much stress cannot be put upon this subject. Speech is golden in its opportunities; it is a pity that a grain of the precious gold should ever be thrown away. Most of us talk too much. Silence is better far than idle, sinful, or foolish speech. Yet there may be idle silence too; our gift of speech was given to us to be used, but it must be used with wisdom. We should never be content to talk even five minutes with another, without saying at least a word or two that may do good, that may give a helpful impulse or kindle an upward aspiration. Even in the lightest, most playful conversation, there may be an opportunity before closing, to drop a serious word that may be remembered.

"Yea, find thou always time to say some earnest word
Between the idle talk, lest with thee henceforth,
Night and day, regret shall walk."

CHAPTER XIII.

ON KEEPING QUIET.

TALKING is good if it be good talking. Very wonderful is the gift of speech, and the power of good words to do good is simply incalculable. But not all talking is good; there are words that are firebrands or daggers. We are responsible, too, for using our tongue. An old proverb tells us that, while speech is silvern, silence is golden. Of course the saying says too much. There are times when silence is not golden, is in fact only base alloy, and when duty can be done only by speaking. We have no right to keep our gentle thoughts and feelings in our heart unexpressed when loved ones are starving for words of affection. We dare not close our lips on an unspoken message from God, or a word of witnessing for God.

Nevertheless, it is ofttimes our duty to be silent. There are times when silence is indeed golden, and when speech is only silvern, or even poor dross. It is a good thing to know when to speak and when not to speak. Some persons talk altogether too much. They chatter on forever. Nothing ever awes them into silence. One tells of standing before a great picture — a picture representing one of the most tender and sacred scenes in the life of Christ. There was everything in the occasion to produce reverence, almost awe. The little group that stood before the picture with uncovered heads were deeply impressed, and spoke, if at all, only to give expression in whispered words to the emotion which possessed them. But in the midst of this worshipful hush there came in another group of visitors. The picture had no subduing effect upon them. They talked on in careless mood, speaking of the mere accessories of the great work of art, evidently without any perception of the real meaning of the painting, or of any of the scenes which it portrayed.

This was an occasion when speech was not only impertinent, trivial, and out of place, but was also irreverent, undevout, and when silence was the only fitting expression of the thoughtful heart.

We may learn much from our Master's example about the duty of silence. No other man ever spoke as he did, such marvellous words, such words of power; but in the Gospel story the silences of Jesus are quite as wonderful as his words. There were thirty silent years at the beginning, out of which only one single sentence is preserved to us. The silence of those years is wonderfully impressive.

We urge young Christian people in these days to be always talking, telling their experiences, witnessing to their love for Christ; we insist that they shall let no meeting pass without "a little word for Jesus." But Jesus himself, with a heart full of love for God and a mind teeming with holy thoughts which he was eager to express, waited thirty years in silence before he began to speak. Perhaps we talk too much about our religion. Perhaps it were better if we waited longer and mused in silence, while the fire burns, until we can speak more wisely and with more power. Then what we say would be something worth while.

There were times, too, when Jesus was silent in the presence of human need and distress. It seems strange to us, as we read the records, that he did not speak when words would have given such comfort and relief. But no doubt silence was better then than speech, or he would have spoken. There are times when kindly words would better be restrained, when even love may be too tender. There are times when we would do our friends harm if we were to lift away or even lighten their burden; because the blessing they need is in the burden, and to remove it would be to rob them of God's gift in it.

Many people talk too much, too, when they find their friends in sorrow. They want to express sympathy; and they think they must go over all the details of the grief with them, and then must expound to them the comforts of the Bible. But there are few places where many words are more unfit than in the presence of grief. A warm pressure of the hand, a word or two of strong sympathy, and a quiet heart's prayer to God for help, will give the truest comfort.

We get from our Master also the lesson of silence under injury or wrong. That is what meekness is — not answering back, not contending for one's rights, not striving against injustice, not resisting insult, but quietly submitting and enduring. Over and over we see Jesus bearing reproaches and injuries in sweet silence. He kept silent about Judas while the treason was ripening. He was silent on his trial, reviled but not reviling again. On his cross he spoke no word of bitterness or of complaint. While the nails were being driven into his hands and feet his only word was a prayer for those who were causing him such anguish.

It is hard to keep quiet when others say bitter or false things to us, or when we are suffering wrongfully. But silence is always better than words in such experiences. If we speak at all, when smarting under a sense of personal injury, we are almost sure to say words we would better not have said. Anger is a kind of insanity. A furious man is a madman in two senses. We pity the dumb, but dumbness is safer and better than ungoverned speech which works havoc all about.

> "I hastily opened my lips
> And uttered a word of disdain
> That wounded a friend and forever estranged
> A heart I would die to regain."

One of the sad things about ill-timed words is that they cannot be recalled. Rose Terry Cooke, in a little poem called, "Unreturning," presents this truth in a very striking way. Flowers fade, but there will be more blossoms. Snow melts, but it will snow again. You may weep over the unkind thing you said which so stung your friend's heart, and your friend may never speak of it to you, nor show in any way that he even remembers it, but the word itself never can be recalled. Then she continues:—

> Never shall thy spoken word
> Be again unsaid, unheard.
> Well its work the utterance wrought,
> Woe or weal—whate'er it brought;
>
> Once for all the rune is read,
> Once for all the judgment said.
> Though it pierced, a poisoned spear,
> Through the soul thou holdest dear;
> Though it quiver, fierce and deep,
> Through some stainless spirit's sleep;
> Idle, vain, the flying sting
> That a passing rage might bring,
> Speech shall give it fangs of steel,
> Utterance all its barb reveal.
>
> Give thy tears of blood and fire,
> Pray with pangs of mad desire,
> Offer life, and soul, and all,
> That one sentence to recall:
> Wrestle with its fatal wrath,
> Chase with flying feet its path;—
> Once for all thy word is sped;
> None evade it but the dead.
> All thy travail will be vain:
> Spoken words come not again.

Surely it is "a time to keep silence" when we are under the pressure of any sense of wrong or injustice, for if we speak then our words will have a sting in them, and an hour later we shall be sure to regret that we spoke at all. The Bible has much to say about keeping quiet, but how may we learn the lesson? Tongue-mastery is not easy. We are assured that even wild beasts are more easily tamed than the human tongue. Yet the tongue is not utterly untamable. The lesson of keeping silence can be learned; and we should never be content until we have learned to be quiet, not speaking, even under the keenest provocation. How can we learn the lesson? Self-discipline is important. We must watch ourselves. We must get the mastery over our own life. We must bring our tongue into subjection, so that it will speak or be silent as we bid it.

But we need divine help. Christ overcame the world, and he is able to overcome every power of evil. There is a secret of Christian faith by which we may put our whole life into Christ's keeping. If we would only wait for him to speak in our words, we should often be silent where now we chatter endlessly.

There is a picture of Augustine and his mother looking up toward heaven in reverent awe. "Oh, that God would speak to us!" he is saying. "Perhaps he is," the mother replies.

If we keep quiet and still, he will speak to us at the right time. Then, unless his voice of gentle stillness speak in us, we would better be silent. Divinely inspired silences are better far than any human words we could speak.

CHAPTER XIV.

LEARNING TO BE THOUGHTFUL.

ONE of the finest things in a complete Christian character is thoughtfulness. It gives a wondrous charm to a life. It makes one a benediction wherever he goes. It tempers all his conduct, softening all natural harshness into gentleness, and giving to his every word and act, and to all his bearing, a spirit of kindliness.

A thoughtful person does not have to be asked to help others — he helps, as it were, instinctively. He is ever ready to do the obliging thing, to say the encouraging word, to show an interest in the life of others, to perform those countless little kindnesses which so brighten the common pathway. He does not make his life an offence to others, a constant irritating influence. He never meddles with other persons' affairs, but respects the individuality and the rights of every one. He curbs his curiosity, and does not pry into matters of which he has no right to know. He is most careful not to touch others at sensitive points. If any one has a physical deformity or any feature which is marred, he is careful in conversation never to refer to it, and seems never to notice it, or to be conscious of it.

Thoughtfulness reveals itself quite as much in what it does not do as in the things it does. Many people make their very goodness so obtrusive as to do harm, and give pain to those they would help. They are too anxious to be helpful. They intrude upon others, pressing their offers of kindness upon them in ways which become, if not offensive and impertinent, at least burdensome. When their friends are in sorrow, they are sincerely eager to give comfort; but they fail to understand the sacredness of grief, or to respect the craving of sad hearts for quiet, and allow their eagerness to become intrusiveness. There is no more delicate test of thoughtfulness than that which sorrow furnishes. Usually love's sweetest and best service then is rendered in the quietest expression of sympathy, certainly with no undue pressing of one's self into the presence of the friends who are in trouble, and with no over-eager offer to help. Then, unless from personal experience of grief one has been prepared for giving effective sympathy, one would better not seek to be a privileged comforter.

Thoughtfulness has a wide field for its ministry in the family circle and in the daily household life. Perhaps few young people come by this grace naturally, are born with it. Usually it has to be learned. Most of us think first of ourselves and our own comfort and convenience, and are not apt to think how our words, acts, and dispositions will affect others. We say what at the moment we feel like saying, not stopping to ask whether it will give pleasure or pain to those who must hear it. We like to say, saying it too with some pride, that we are plain, frank people, honest and outspoken, not indulging in courtly phrases, but sincere though brusque, not realizing that our brusqueness and plainness ofttimes hurt gentle hearts. We do the thing we feel inclined to do, because it pleases us, not remembering that true love seeks not its own, but thinks first of the comfort and pleasure of others.

Without being aware of it, many of us are miserably selfish in our life among others. We practically forget that there are any other people, or that we ought to make any sacrifices, or practise any self-denials, for their sake. Young people at home, for example, will indulge themselves in sleep in the mornings, coming down late to breakfast, not thinking of the trouble they cause to those who have to do the work, nor how they interfere with the order of the household. Thoughtfulness seeks never to add to another's burdens, never to make extra work or care, but always to lighten loads.

In much home conversation, too, there is a lack of thoughtfulness shown. Not always is the speech gentle — sometimes it is sharp and bitter, even rude. Playfulness is to be allowed, and in every family there should be a readiness to take a jest without being hurt by it. Over-sensitiveness is a serious fault. Some persons are so touchy as to demand an excessive thoughtfulness — a watchfulness in all our relations with these over-gentle souls which is unreasonable, which makes friendship with them a burden. Life is too short, and has too many real duties and cares, for us to be held to such exactions of attention and kindness as these good people would demand. Yet always in our relations with others there should be that refined courtesy which is part of the lesson of love that we learn from our Master — "As I have loved you." Rude words never should be spoken, even in jest.

Thoughtfulness will seek always to say kindly words, never words that will give pain, but ever those that will give pleasure. We have no right, for the sake of saying a bright thing, to let loose a shaft, however polished, that will make a loving heart bleed. Mr. Sill says: —

> These clumsy feet, still in the mire,
>   Go crushing blossoms without end:
> These hard, well-meaning hands we thrust
>   Among the heart-strings of a friend.
>
> The ill-timed truth we might have kept —
>   Who knows how sharp it pierced and stung?
> The word we have not sense to say —
>   Who knows how grandly it had rung?

These are fragments of a lesson which might be indefinitely extended. Are you thoughtful? — that is the question. Answer it for yourself. Some one has said, "Unless our religion has sweetened us to a very considerable extent — giving us the control of our temper, checked us in our moments of irritation and weakness, enabled us to meet misfortune and, in a measure, overcome it, developed within us the virtues of patience and long-suffering, making us tender and charitable in our judgments of others, and generally diffusing about us an atmosphere that is genial and winsome, — whatever else we may have gained, one thing is sure, religion is not having its perfect work in us; and, even though our Christian life is clear and positive, it is only as a gnarled and twisted apple-tree that bears no fruit, only as a prickly bush that bears no roses, and the very thing which of all others we should have is the very thing in which we are most deficient. A Christian life without sweetness is a lamp without light, salt without savor."

We all know in our own experience the value of sincere and Christly thoughtfulness. We do not like to come in contact with thoughtlessness. We know well how it hurts and how unbeautiful, how unchristian, it seems when we see it in another, and when our heart is the one that suffers from its harsh, rude impact. We all long for thoughtfulness; our hearts hunger and thirst for it. It is bread and wine to us.

> "We long for tenderness like that which hung
>   About us, lying on our mother's breast;
> Unselfish feeling, that no pen or tongue
>   Can praise aright since silence sings it best;
> A love as far removed from passion's heat
>   As from the chillness of its dying fire;
> A love to lean on when the falling feet
>   Begin to totter and the eyes to tire.
> In youth's bright hey-day hottest love we seek,
>   The reddest rose we grasp; but when it dies,

> God grant that later blossoms, violets meek,
>   May spring for us beneath life's autumn skies;
> God grant some loving one be near to bless
> Our weary way with simple tenderness!"

What we long for in others, in their relation to us, we should be ready to give to them. What in others hurts us, gives us pain, we ought to avoid in our contact with others. Thoughtfulness is one of the finest, ripest fruits of love, and all who would be like the Master must seek to learn this lesson and wear this grace.

CHAPTER XV.

ON THE CONTROL OF TEMPER.

A GREAT many people seem to have trouble with their temper. Some years since an English philosopher undertook an investigation. He arranged that about two thousand persons should be put unconsciously under watchful eyes for a certain period, and that a study should be made of their temper. A tabulation of the reports showed that more than one-half of the two thousand were bad-tempered in various ways and degrees. Almost every adjective qualifying temper of an unlovely kind was used in defining the various shades and phases of unloveliness which were found to exist in the persons under inspection.

It is not pleasant to believe that more than one-half of the people about us are so defective in the matter of temper. It is a comfort to know, however, that about forty-eight per cent are good-tempered in various degrees. Yet the fact that the preponderance is on the wrong side is humiliating.

Many Christian people are willing to confess to an ungentle temper. They seem to think it, too, a matter of not very grave importance. Perhaps the very commonness of the infirmity blinds our eyes to its unbeauty and its sinfulness. We are apt to regard the malady more as a weakness than as something which makes us guilty before God.

But there is no question that bad temper is unchristlike. We cannot think of Jesus as acrimonious, touchy, irritable, peevish, or vindictive. Love ruled all his dispositions, his words, his feelings. He was put to the sorest tests, but never failed. He endured all manner of wrongs, insults, hurts; but, like those flowers which yield their sweetest perfume only when crushed, his life gave out the more sweetness the more it was exposed to men's rudeness and unkindness. We are like Christ only in the measure in which we have the patience, gentleness, and good-temper of Christ.

We all agree that bad temper is very unlovely in other people; it cannot be any more lovely in us as we appear to others' eyes.

> "Search thine own heart. What paineth thee
> In others in thyself may be;
> All dust is frail, all flesh is weak :
> Be thou the true man thou dost seek."

We know, too, what discomfort and pain a bad temper causes wherever the person goes. One form of the malady is sulking. No doubt it is better to pout in silence than to go about spitting out angry words. It was arranged among the sisters of a certain family, that if one of them was in a bad humor she would go to her room, and stay there until she had worked off the unhappy mood, and was fit to be in society again. It would be well if such an arrangement could be made in other homes. A sulking temper, however, does not make such havoc of happiness and comfort in others as a spitfire temper does. An unbridled tongue at the mercy of an ungoverned temper scatters abroad coals of fire and sharp arrows which cause pain and anguish wherever they fly.

It is easy enough to portray the unloveliness of bad temper, and describe the hurt and mischief wrought by its manifestations; we would better address ourselves, however, to the question, How to get a sweet temper. One who finds himself possessed by an unlovely spirit should not be content to go a day longer without beginning the conquest and the culture which will transform the hateful disposition into something Christlike and beautiful.

The first thing to remember is that the change

can be wrought. You may say that you were born with a hasty temper, that you inherited it from both your father and mother. Very likely. Parents do not know what evil heritage they are transmitting to their children when they fail to control their own feelings and tongues; nor what a training-school for strife and irritability they are conducting in their home, when they indulge in bickerings and contentions in the sacred place where only love and patience should have sway.

But suppose that you have received your unhappy temper as a heritage, or have been trained into the habit in your home; you are not to conclude that you have no responsibility in the matter, or that you must stay, in despairing content, just as you are until the end of your days. Because one happens to be born with a faulty disposition is not a reason why one must live and die with it. The essential teaching of Christianity is that human nature can be changed. The worst temper can be schooled into the most divine sweetness of spirit. The tongue which no man can tame Christ can tame, so that, instead of bitterness, it shall give out only love.

It is a great step in the right direction to know that one can get such a victory. One who is aware of his infirmity of temper, and is ashamed and sick of it, should never say, "I cannot help it. It cannot be cured. I must go through life a slave to this miserable habit." A Christian may be more than conqueror over every weakness and everything sinful in himself. All Christ's strength and victory are upon his side to help him to be victorious. Indeed, if he is a true Christian, he will never cease in his efforts to grow like his Master, until at last he is presented faultless before the divine presence in exceeding joy.

The first thing is to know clearly what is to be accomplished, and to determine that the beautiful ideal must certainly be reached. It is a great thing to have in one's soul a vision of perfection toward which one is to grow, and which is one day surely to be reached.

> "There grows in every heart as a shrine
> The giant image of perfection."

What God puts into our heart as a vision he will help us to realize if we do our part. However, the lesson is not to be learned in a day; it will probably take you years to master it. But a little part of it should be got each day, one line added to the picture. Paul was quite an old man when he said he had learned in whatsoever state he was therein to be content. His language implies also that it was not easy for him to learn this lesson, and that he had not attained full proficiency in it until he had reached old age. The lesson of sweet temper is probably quite as hard as that of contentment. It has to be learned, too, for it does not come naturally to many of us. But it can be learned. We need only to put ourselves into the school of Christ and stay there, accepting his teaching and discipline, and advancing little by little, until at last we can say, "I have learned in whatever circumstances I am, under whatever provocation, irritation, or temptation to anger or impatience, always to keep sweet-tempered."

Self-control is really the heart of the lesson. Temper is not a bad quality; temper is an element of strength. A person without temper is weak, soft, pliable, lacks spirit. The problem is not to crush or destroy temper, but to get the mastery of it, so as to be able to endure annoyance, wrong, insult, and not get angry, nor speak unadvisedly. Young people should school themselves continually in self-control. A really strong man is one with strong passions and affections, which are held in complete mastery. This is the secret of a good temper.

Then we can get help from Christ. In his own disciple family there was one who at the first was hasty, fiery, and vindictive, but who at length grew into such sweet beauty of disposition and character that he was known as the beloved disciple, the disciple of love. John learned his lesson by lying on the bosom of Jesus. Intimacy with Christ, close, personal friendship with him, living near his heart of love, will transform the most unloving, undisciplined nature into sweetness of spirit.

But there is more than even friendship, with its holy influence; Christ lives in the heart of every one who will admit him. Every true Christian is by right a temple of the Holy Ghost. If you let this holy guest dwell in you, he will transfigure you from within by the renewing of your mind. He will fill your heart with love, — love that behaveth not itself unseemly, that is not provoked; love that is patient, thoughtful, gentle, kind. Such love within the heart will soon get control of all the outer life, — the dispositions, the speech, the manners, and all the expression of the inner life. Thus bitterness, wrath, clamor, and all evil speaking will give place to gentleness, goodness, and grace.

Of course we have a part and a responsibility

in all this. We must accept the divine teaching, and receive the divine help. We must let the word of Christ dwell in us, let the peace of God rule us, let Christ himself live in us.

Every one of us should accept now the lesson of sweet temper which the Master sets, and should never intermit his diligence until the lesson is perfectly learned. That is the way God works in us; he sets the task for us, and then as we try to learn it he helps us.

CHAPTER XVI.

GETTING ALONG WITH PEOPLE.

ONE of the earliest experiences of life is the realizing that there are other people. It comes to the child when it first discovers that its freedom is limited by the will of another. It cannot always have its own way. It finds its will opposed and its pleasure interrupted. Other people have something to say about the carrying out of its little plans.

At every point as we go on into the thickening experiences of life, the lesson of living with others meets us. It is not alway easy to accept gracefully these contacts with others, and to enter into kindly relations with them. There are some persons who seem to be very good alone, while no one comes near them, while no other life touches theirs, when they have to think of no one but themselves, who make wretched business of living when they come into personal relations with others. Then they are selfish, tyrannical, despotic, wilful, exacting. They will not yield to any other one's desire or necessity. They must have their own way; and they drive their life like a rough ploughshare right through the comfort, the desire, the feelings, of others.

It seems almost a pity there could not be a few corners fenced off in this great world for such people as these, where they could live altogether alone, with no one ever to interfere with their rights or liberties, or to impinge in any way upon their comfort. But this is not God's ordinance for human lives. We are to live together in families, in communities, in friendship's circle. Indeed, no worse fate could befall us than to be doomed to live alone. We might thus be absolved from the duties of love, we could then have our own way, we should not be required to think of anybody but ourselves, and there would be no call for self-denial or sacrifice; but, meanwhile, we should be growing into monsters of selfishness. We never can learn love's lessons save in life's school, where the lessons are set for us in actual human relations.

It certainly costs to live with people. We have to give up many of our own preferences to please them. We have to deny ourselves many enjoyments, so as not to give them pain. The price of living with others sweetly and harmoniously is self-forgetfulness, self-effacement. But this cost is the very gold of life. It is the only antidote for selfishness. It is the way of Christlikeness. People are means of grace to us in many ways, and not in the smallest degree through the self-denials which we are required to make in living with them. It is the self-discipline of friendship and home and human fellowship that makes men and women of us, that makes us like Christ.

I used to pity those whom I saw in circumstances in which they were compelled to bear heavy burdens for others, to serve, to sacrifice, to deny themselves, in fulfilling love's duties; but I have learned to look upon such persons with deep interest as privileged scholars in Christ's school. If the lessons set for them are hard, the mastering of the lessons advances them in the rank of character. That is God's way of making Christly men and women.

But the problem before us now is how to get along with other people. There are instances in which there is scarcely any problem here at all; the other people have learned the patience and love of Christ so well that anybody could live with them. They will not quarrel, they never stand up for their rights, they would rather suffer almost any wrong than resist.

Even a selfish and tyrannical man could get along with them, for they meekly let him have his own way.

But usually the problem is not so easily solved. Other people want our recognition, claim their rights, resist encroachments, demand of us attention, respect, service. Then some people are touchy, easily provoked, always watching for slights, like tinder only waiting for a spark to start the fire. Some are obstinate and unyielding, heady, unwilling to give up their own opinion or their own way. The average people are probably like ourselves — little better, little worse, about as hard to live with as we are — probably no harder.

The lesson set for us teaches us that we must not only live with people, but must live lovingly with them. This applies to all sorts and conditions of men, not the gentle and peaceable only, but the rude and quarrelsome as well. We are to love our enemies, to do good to those who treat us unkindly. The problem of Christian living is always to keep the heart sweet, the manner gracious and loving, and the hand outstretched for service, wherever we may be.

How can we do this? To begin with, we must have the spirit of love. We need to get the true definition of love, too, that we may know what it requires. Love is not an easy sentiment. To love, according to the New Testament, is a very costly duty. Love suffereth long and is kind. Love seeketh not its own, is not provoked, taketh not account of evil, beareth all things, endureth all things.

We may break up the lesson into parts. We need patience in living with others. Patience implies suffering, — keeping quiet and sweet when it is not easy to do so, enduring pain without repining or murmuring, accepting wrong and injustice without resentment. Impatience never can get along peacefully with other people; but patience moves amid the greatest complexity of tastes, dispositions, and feelings, undisturbed. We all know some one who carries out this spirit. Perhaps it is in a home where it is not easy to practise the lesson of love; but there this gentle spirit dwells with almost angelic sweetness — quiet, suffering long. The more there is to suffer, the sweeter is this patient spirit.

The spirit of service is another secret of living together happily. One who demands that others must show him deference, doing things for him, serving him, has not learned the true art of living with others. If he assumes this attitude to those about him, they will assume the same attitude toward him. The result at the best will be a sort of armed neutrality. But if one assumes toward others the spirit of loving service, the desire to help and serve, he has solved the problem. It was thus that Jesus himself lived among men—he came "not to be ministered unto, but to minister." His thought of others was, not what he might have them do for him, but what he might do for them, how he might help them, how he might advance their interests, how he might give them comfort or relief. If we relate ourselves to others in this way, we shall get on happily with them. Love begets love. Serving softens hearts and changes lives.

Another secret of getting on well with others is to honor them, to expect noble and beautiful things of them, to set as our aim to bring out the best that is in them. Margaret Fuller said that all the good she had ever done to others she had done by calling on every nature for its best. To do this we do not need to flatter others, to appeal to their vanity by saying always complimentary things; and yet there is fine grace in having a pleasing word to say to every one, a word that will honor him, and also inspire him to do beautiful things. The best way to do a man good is to expect good of him. If we always call on others for their best, we also make it easier to live with them; for we see them through kindly eyes, and are patient with their faults and frailties.

Thoughtfulness is another of the secrets of happy living with others. Most young people begin life without this grace. They do not naturally think of others, or modify their own conduct for the sake of others. A boy goes through the house wearing his great heavy boots, singing at the top of his voice, utterly heedless of the fact that his mother is sick in her room, and that his noise almost kills her. Thoughtfulness has to be learned, but when it is learned it is a marvellous sweetener of associated life. Thoughtful people never speak the careless word that cuts to the heart. They avoid the unpleasant theme of conversation. They are careful not to say anything that would excite anger or resentment. They are ready ever with the right word at the right time, and they come always with their sympathy and kindness when the need is greatest. We never can get on well with others without thoughtfulness; but with this beautiful grace we are prepared to live in almost any condition without friction or irritation.

Another essential is good temper. Love is not provoked. It beareth all things and always keeps sweet. Some persons have a reserve of good nature which serves them well when others are disposed to get angry. They say some pleasant word which proves to be the soft answer that turneth away wrath. Put two touchy people together, and they will not easily learn the lesson of living in companionship. They will learn it if they are Christians; but it will not be done easily, nor without much cost and pain to both. In any case, however, a happy, cheerful temper is a wonderful sweetener of fellowship. We all are human; and there are few of us who at best do not say words, or do things, which give pain to those closest to us. Even true love is not always just and kind. Then it is that love must outdo love — the one who has been hurt must show love's long-suffering, overcoming evil with good.

These are mere suggestions concerning the problem, how to live sweetly in relations with others. Young people are sometimes rash and hot-headed; and it is not so easy for such to live together in love as it is for those who are older, who have learned more lessons, whose hearts have been softened by life's experiences. The young are less ready to yield their own way. They are apt to be wilful and hasty. There is all the more reason, therefore, why young people should take up this lesson as one that must be learned if they would make much of their life. For if it is said of any one that other people cannot live with him, it is evident that something is seriously wrong with his life. It should be the aim of all, as much as lieth in them, to live peaceably with all others. They should practise self-restraint, humility, self-renunciation, the law of loving service, patience, good temper, and all the Christian graces, so that their life shall be a benediction to all whom they touch.

CHAPTER XVII.

THE MATTER OF SOCIAL DUTIES.

There are two extremes in the matter of sociability. One is to want to be with others all the time, never to be alone. There are girls who must either always have company or be company. They do not seem to themselves to be living unless they are chattering with somebody. There are young fellows who never spend an evening at home. When the day's duties are ended, as soon as they can hurry through their evening meal, they are off to meet some one, or to attend some entertainment. That is one way.

The other is the unsocial way, never to go anywhere, nor to receive others at one's own home. Young persons who adopt this course are sometimes book-worms. They are eager to read and study; and they regard every minute spent in society, or in showing hospitality, as lost time, time stolen and wasted. Or if they are not book-worms they may be shy people, who cannot meet others without embarrassment

THE MATTER OF SOCIAL DUTIES. 125

and shrink from all social contacts. So from sheer timidity they stay at home, perhaps not doing anything worth while, but merely avoiding meeting others.

Or it may be through dislike to society. Many people are bored by company. People do not interest them. The conversation of the parlor wearies them. They feel themselves under no obligation to entertain others, or to put brightness and cheer into their hearts. They enjoy uninterrupted quiet more than any general companionship. For these or other reasons there are persons who avoid company as far as possible. They prefer to be alone rather than with others.

Neither of these two ways of regarding social duties is the ideal way. To be out on the street or in company continually, is to neglect duties to one's self and to one's home which come in among first obligations. On the other hand, to keep altogether to one's self, away from people, is to neglect duties which one owes to others, and at the same time to miss opportunities for self-culture which can be gotten only in contact with other lives.

Young people cannot afford to let drop out of their life regular habits of reading and study. Their education is not finished, however well they may have mastered the curriculum of the schools through which they have passed. The best school only puts a bundle of keys into the pupils' hands, even at graduation. With these magic keys they can open many treasures of knowledge. But they fail to make any true and worthy use of their education, if, on leaving school, they shut up their books, and at the same time close the doors of their mind, and cease to add to their store of knowledge. The object of their education is to prepare them for reading and thinking intelligently.

Every young person, therefore, should form and courageously and persistently maintain regular habits of reading and study. This will require the setting apart of certain hours of each week when company must be excluded, when one must be alone with one's books. It will not do to leave this duty to any haphazard chance, taking up a book, the book that lies nearest, merely whenever there may be an unoccupied hour. The only way to make anything worth while of reading is to do it systematically, to put one's self under rigid rules in the matter. If young people are busy during the day, hours must be taken in the evenings. If they would grow in intelligence and advance in self-culture, they must be content to give to society only a proper proportion of time, putting self-improvement always first.

Christian young people have duties also to their church. These will require at least one evening each week. There is an old proverb which says, "Prayer and provender hinder no man's journey." Anything else would better be left out of life than one's religious duties. Self-culture is the highest of all culture. To forget God is to cut one's self off from the source of all joy, blessing, and good. Yet one is not required to give all one's spare hours to religious meetings. There should be daily spiritual exercises, the keeping unbroken of one's relation with God; but this does not involve daily public services. We can soon run our soul very thin by going continually to meetings. Bible study is essential to true spiritual culture, and the best Bible study is usually in the closet. We should so order our life that we shall have daily silent times, when we can let the words of God speak themselves into our heart. It is the blessing which comes in such quiet moments that prepares us for the life we must live outside, in the face of the world.

The young people have duties to their own families which should keep them much at home. There is something wrong with the girl who is restless when she is not out somewhere, who never has time for long quiet talks with her mother, whom home duties irk and tire, and who is happy only when she is with her young friends outside. There is something wrong with the young man who never wants to spend an evening or an hour quietly with his own family. If the home is happy and true, the young folks in it can have no sweeter enjoyments than those they may find within their own doors, with no stranger to intermeddle. Then they owe it to their loved ones to bring their share of fellowship and brightness into the home life. It is not fair to keep all one's cheer for others, robbing those who deserve the best one has to give.

These are suggestions of duties on one side. Young persons cannot afford to give all their time and interest to social matters. But there are duties which we owe to society. The rule of Christian love requires us to think of the things of others as well as of those which concern ourselves. We owe a debt to every one who comes within the range of our influence. We are commanded to please others for their good, to edification. An unsocial person is not showing the best there is in religion. Love is cordial, kindly, sympathetic, obliging.

It makes the disposition sunny. The truest Christian has the kindliest interest in others.

Jesus was always ready to give himself to men. While he often spent his nights apart with God, and had his hours when he hid away from men, yet he went among the people freely, and was a wonderful dispenser of cheer, comfort, and kindness. We should train ourselves to be in the world as he was. We should not selfishly withhold our life from those who need it. We should carry out to others the blessing and the good we get for ourselves in the quiet of our study, or in the sweetness of our home fellowships. We are to be dispensers of God's good gifts. What we receive, and would keep for ourselves only, will not avail for good even to us; for we really have only what we give. Keeping for ourselves only is losing. Hence no young person should be a recluse, shutting himself away from others, on the ground that he must devote all his time to self-improvement. He owes a debt to others which he can pay only by going among others.

Of course, it follows that one's social influence should be always good, refining, inspiring, uplifting. It is a serious thing to touch another life if the touch be not in blessing. There are young people whose influence is unwholesome. They do not make others better, happier, truer, richer-hearted. They lead toward lower planes of living, not higher; they are of the earth, earthy.

This is not a proper use to make of one's life. It is possible, however, for young people to do much good in their social relations, not by preaching, but by sweet neighborly living. They may be so true, so courteous, so thoughtful, so helpful, that even in hours of play and amusement their influence shall be refining and wholesome. That should be the intent of all Christian influence.

Hospitality is a Christian duty. We are exhorted in Holy Scripture to be ready to entertain strangers, since by doing so some have entertained angels unawares. Some people say they have not time for hospitality; that duties press too urgently; that guests in the home interrupt the order of the household life. Some busy Christian men think, too, that they must shut themselves away from calls. But it can only be with twofold loss that one declines the privilege of showing hospitality, — the losing of countless opportunities of doing good, and the loss to one's self of the good which "angels unawares" bring when they come. Not many young people can plead that they are too busy to see such as come to them; and they cannot know the value of a cordial welcome to those who come, nor can they estimate the blessing to themselves that even a stranger, received in the name of Christ, may bring to them.

Thus there are social duties which one may not refuse to perform; they are binding and incumbent. Then, to shut ourselves away from others is not only to withhold the blessing we owe to them; it is also to rob ourselves of great good which we can get only through wholesome contact with other lives. Without being sanctimonious or priggish, we should make even our social relations opportunities of being helpful.

CHAPTER XVIII.

THE USE OF TIME.

IF you saw a man standing by the shore, and flinging gold coins and diamonds into the sea, you would say he was insane. Yet the angels see many people continually doing something very like this. Not gold and precious stones do they thus throw away, but minutes, hours, days, weeks, and years of time, — possessions which are of greater worth than any coins and gems of earth.

> " Come, gone — gone forever,
> Gone as an unreturning river, —
> To-morrow, to-day, yesterday, never,
> Gone once for all."

If we knew the intrinsic value of time to us, we would not allow a moment of it ever to be wasted. It is said that in the mints, where money is coined, the sweepings of the floors are gathered and passed through the fire, and that in the course of a year large amounts of gold are saved from the mere dust of the precious metal which flies from it as it passes through the various processes of minting. What vast values would be saved if there were some way of gathering up all the little fragments of the days and hours, the golden dust of time, which people let drop amid the wastes!

Then think how much most of us would really add to the length of our life if we had learned to use every hour and moment. We talk pathetically of the brevity of life. We are often heard complaining about the shortness of the days, wishing they had many more hours in them. Probably the majority of persons who live seventy-five years could have doubled their span — living practically one hundred and fifty years — if they had only used their time with wise economy, and had not squandered any of it. This is only saying that they have wasted one-half of their time, and have made only one-half as much of their life as they might have done.

There are many ways in which time is wasted. There is a great deal more resting than is necessary. There is an impression that a few hours' work gives one a right to rest all the other hours of the twenty-four. Every one must rest. There are divine ordinances which call us to rest. We spend about one-third of our time in sleep. Sleep is necessary; the hours given to it are not wasted, although some sleep more than is necessary. God gives blessings to his beloved in sleep, — blessings of renewal of strength, the refilling of the exhausted fountains of life. Our Sabbaths take one-seventh of our whole life, but time spent in true Sabbath-keeping is not wasted. Then, time must be given to eating, to physical exercise, to home fellowships, to friendships, to religious services, private and public, and to reading and study.

But time thus used is not lost or wasted. This resting is as much a part of our real living as actual work is. Yet there are many persons who fail to get the most from their hours of recreation. The best rest is not absolute idleness, but occupation that calls into play a class of faculties which are not active in one's ordinary work. There are those who, after busy days in some trade or business or other calling, find several hours every evening for reading good books. Thus they add continually to the quality of their life, keeping in exercise a very important part of their nature, enriching their character, and preparing themselves for larger influence and greater usefulness.

THE USE OF TIME.

There are many ways of wasting time. Many really busy people waste a great deal of time in little fragments — five minutes here, ten minutes there, half an hour to-day, and an hour to-morrow. Those who understand the true value of time, and have learned the secret of using it, always have something worth while to fill up all the little interstices. They have a book to read when they find a few minutes to spare before a meal is ready, or when waiting for one on whom they have called to appear, in the railway station waiting for the train, or on any occasion of delay. Time is well spent in which we get a beautiful thought, an important fact or a suggestion of a lesson into our mind.

Or the fragments of time may be filled with little acts of helpfulness or kindness. You are travelling. You cannot read all the time. But there are persons travelling with you to whom perhaps you may properly introduce yourself. You may lay down your book for a little quiet talk with a seatmate or a fellow-passenger. There are lives which carry ever afterward the memory and the influence of little talks with strangers on a railway train or in a stage-coach or on a steamer. If one's heart be full of the love of Christ, there is no limit to the blessing one may be in this way. Thus the moments, instead of being wasted in idle dreaming, may be given something to keep which they will bring back at judgment day multiplied a thousand-fold.

A writer tells of an English nobleman, who, when he went over his estate, always carried acorns in his pocket; and when he found a bare spot, he would plant one of them. By and by there would be a tree growing on the place, adorning it. So we may plant on every empty space of time a seed of something beautiful, which will not only be an adornment, but will prove a blessing to others. It is one of the finest secrets of life to know how to redeem the minutes from waste, and to make them bearers of blessing, of cheer, of encouragement, of good, to others.

No time given to service of love is wasted, even though nothing seems to come of it. Some persons are discouraged in their efforts to do good because so much of their kindness seems to be in vain. But no good deed or word is really lost. Sometime, somewhere, the blessing will appear. If the one you sought to help is not helped, some other one may be instead. Then the whole world is sweeter because of every kindness done or good word spoken. Charles Kingsley says,—

There is no failure for the good or wise;
What though thy seed should fall by the wayside,
And the birds snatch it? Yet the birds are fed;
Or they may bear it far across the tide
To give rich harvest after thou art dead.

Much time is wasted in useless occupation, in doing things which are not worth while. No sin is worth while — rather, it is the sowing of a curse, not only in the world, but also in the heart of him who does the sinful thing. Time spent in sin is far worse than wasted. Then, there are other things which are not regarded as sins, but which are of no value to any one, and bring no benefit to him who spends his time in doing them. There is a great deal of reading that is not worth while. You go through book after book, and from all the pages get not one enriching thought, one helpful inspiration, one suggestion of beauty, one impulse toward a better life. All you have at the end of a year of such reading is only a confused memory of exciting sensations, unwholesome incidents, and unreal experiences. You would better have spent the time in sleep or in sheer idleness than in going through such worthless books.

There is altogether too much of such reading done. There are good novels, great works of fiction, which teach splendid lessons, which show magnificent character and noble conduct, which inspire their readers to truer, better living. But there are novels which give unworthy and unwholesome thoughts of life, which leave in the mind of readers a residuum of unholy thoughts, false ideals, the trail of the serpent. Then there are novels which, if they are not positively evil in their spirit and tendency, are inane, senseless, with nothing in them to make any one truer, braver, or sweeter-spirited.

A great deal of the popular reading of our day is but a waste of time, if not worse. If instead of it people would read only that which is worth while, how much richer they would be at the end of their life!

These are only suggestions of ways of using and wasting time. No problem that comes before us is more important than this — what to do with time. It is a young people's problem, too; because in youth, if ever, we learn how to live. The habits we form then will go with us to the end of our days. If we learn then the value of moments, and form the habit of giving every minute something worthy to keep, we shall have found the secret of living in threescore and ten years full tenscore years of such life as most people live.

CHAPTER XIX.

THE MAKING OF A MAN.

THIS world is not a place merely to live in, nor a place in which to do certain kinds of business; it is a great workshop in which to make men.

It is not easy for us to be good and to grow into beautiful life. Even God does not find it easy to make us into noble character. It is not hard to take a lump of clay, and shape it into any form we desire. It is fairly easy to take a piece of soft wood, and carve it into a figure of beauty. It is harder to cut a block of marble into a form of loveliness, for the stone is hard. But it is harder still to take a block of humanity, and make it into a man, bearing the divine image. Yet that is what God is doing with every human life that lies in his hands.

A baby is not a man. It may be very beautiful and sweet, and may have folded up in its life many fine possibilities; but it is only a baby. All its lessons have yet to be learned, its powers have yet to be developed, the capacities that lie folded up in its hand and brain and heart have yet to be brought out and trained, its character has to be fashioned into loveliness and strength. The education begins at once, with the mother for teacher and the home for schoolroom; but the process must be slow, and it will require a long time.

As the child gets older, other teachers come in and do their work, and the sphere of the education widens. The boy goes to school, perhaps by and by to college. At last he is graduated, or finishes his apprenticeship or his training, and takes hold of life's duties for himself. But the man is not yet made. He has reached an important stage in life. He takes his place among men. Burdens and responsibilities are put upon him.

Now he begins to learn the deeper lessons of life—begins to learn how to live. The principles he has adopted for himself are now to be tested in practice. His theories of duty he is now to work out in every-day experience. His character is to be tried, and by the strain upon it is to be fashioned and wrought into fixedness and permanency. Life itself is now the school, and the conditions and experiences of life are the teachers.

Now it is seen how the training the young

man has received in the schools of his youth has fitted him for real life. Perhaps he has wasted his time and missed his lessons; if so, he will find himself unequal to the duties which come into his hands. Perhaps he has failed in acquiring self-discipline, or has not gathered into his life the strength of moral principle; if so, he will fail in the stress of temptation, and will not stand the testing of character which every young man must meet when he enters the world's battles.

Now it is that the real making of the man begins. All that has gone before has been preliminary and preparatory. It is in duty, in burden-bearing, in struggle, in temptation, in joy and sorrow, in prosperity and adversity, in ease and hardship, in pleasure and pain, in health and sickness, in life's experiences of all kinds, that the work goes on. Everywhere lessons are set which must be learned, if the result in character-building is to be satisfactory.

Take patience, for example. The etymology of the word shows that it is not an easy lesson to learn. It implies suffering, endurance. It is in the bearing of pain, trial, wrong, or hardship, that patience is developed. One definition is, "The character or habit of mind that enables us to suffer afflictions, calamity, provocation, or other evil, with a calm, unruffled temper; endurance without murmuring or fretfulness; calmness; composure."

A young person may have had very little opportunity to learn patience. He has had only ease and his own way, without sickness, disappointment, or pain, with almost no wish ungranted, no desire ungratified, no craving unmet. How will he behave in sickness, in sorrow, or in pain? How will he endure injury, injustice, and wrong? How will he stand the test of disappointment, defeat, or failure? What will be the effect on him of unpleasant contacts with other men? Will he prove patient in such antagonisms? Will he always keep sweet?

Patience is only one of the lessons; there are many more which go to the making of a man. Courage is one. In every scheme of manly character courage is set down as a fundamental quality. All the world scorns cowardice. The highest courage is not physical, merely, but moral. There are men whose faces grow pale in presence of danger, but who, nevertheless, stand firm in their place, or move on in the path of duty without faltering. True moral courage shows itself in devotion to principle, in faithful adherence to the right, in the consecration of the life to common duties, and in the resisting of temptation.

But courage, too, is a lesson set for us, and one which must be learned. We are not all born brave, at least morally brave. The lesson should be taught in the home and in life's first schools. Young people themselves, so soon as they become conscious of the nobleness of courage and the unworthiness of cowardice, should take up the lesson and master it. The way to do this is to hold one's self resolutely and unflinchingly to all heroic and manly conduct in every experience. Bravery is not bluster — quietness is a better test of heroism, ofttimes, than noise. It is in rigid self-discipline that this manly quality is gained and wrought into the character.

Another of the elements in a true man is gentleness — a man must be a gentleman. This includes all the fine feelings wrought into life. The noblest types of manliness the world has ever seen have been marked by womanly gentleness. Jesus was the ideal man; and he would not even break a bruised reed, so gentle was he. Heartlessness is unmanliness, amid whatsoever other great qualities it may be found.

This lesson, too, must be learned. The gentle touch must be gotten by training. The secret is in refinement of feeling. The love which is taught in the New Testament makes one gentle. Every one who would make a true man of himself must cultivate gentleness, both as a spirit in his heart and as a trait in his disposition, his words, his conduct, his acts.

These are a few of the qualities which must always go to the making of a man. Young people must not think that they will naturally grow into fine character, without any care of their own; the natural drift of life is the other way — away from manliness. Only training and self-discipline will yield the noble product. Through all the years the education must go on. Every day brings its new lesson. Every experience has its mission in the building and adorning of the character.

The lesson in all this is that experiences alone will not make a worthy and noble man out of any one. Several things are essential in order that beauty may be wrought out in life's school. The preparation must be right. A misspent youth, with squandered privileges, insures failure in life. Every day and hour of youth must be well spent if one is to be ready for manhood.

The true meaning of experiences must be understood. Many lives are hurt and marred by the things which are intended to fashion them into beauty and strength. We must meet all experiences victoriously.

Then we need Christ at every point. To leave Christ out of life is to thrust away the only hand which can make circumstances minister to the building up of character. Without Christ, apart from him, only marring can come. If we have Christ in all our life, we shall grow into his beauty.

CHAPTER XX.

ON KEEPING UP THE IDEAL.

SOME one says that the sentence, "That will do," has done more harm than any other sentence in the English language. It indicates the acceptance of a standard below the highest. A person has done something which is not his best. He recognizes the fact; but he is too indolent to do it over again, or he is impatient to get the matter off his hands, and decides to let it go as it is. "That will do," is a confession of unworthiness in what is done, and of indolence in the person who does it. He knows he could do better, but decides to let it pass.

Yet this miserable sentence is the ruling motto of many persons' lives. They never do the best they might do. Their whole life is slipshod. They began as children in school, doing barely well enough to pass. They never aimed to excel. They had no ambition to be first or to do perfect work. It was the same on the playground as in the schoolroom — they were satisfied to drag through the game, playing only passably well. They never put quite their whole soul into anything they did.

Thus habits of easy satisfaction were formed in their early years, and they have gone through life with the same unworthy spirit. They know they are not working up to their best, but it does not worry them. They have learned to say at every point, "That will do;" and this covers up the delinquencies and apologizes for the failures.

All the standards of life are affected by it. Conduct is not what it should be. A man knows he is not doing what is really right, that his act would not bear the scrutiny of a rigid judgment; but he says indolently, "Oh, that will do," and so passes over the matter without further compunction. Next time it is easier to fall below the mark; and so the trend is ever downward, until conscience ceases to sting and chide.

A man's work or business also is affected by this spirit. He is content with small achievements and low attainments. He knows he is not accomplishing what he might accomplish, but it costs less to do things in this easy-going way than to do them well, and he soon gets used to the low standard. So it comes about that the man who might have made a splendid mark for himself in his profession, in his business, or in his trade, never rises above a pitiable mediocrity. "That will do" has soothed his languishing enthusiasm into a sleep, out of which nothing ever can wholly awaken it.

Young people should train themselves from childhood never to be satisfied with anything but the very best they can do. A much better maxim to rule them would be, "The good is the enemy of the best." The good should not be enough; nothing should satisfy but the best. Children should begin in school by mastering every lesson, and keeping a high standard in all their studies. Then in their conduct and behavior they should be most rigid with themselves, exacting the strictest truth in word and act, the whitest purity in motive, thought, and feeling, and the utmost sincerity and faithfulness in all their relations with others. In whatever they do they should be satisfied with nothing less than their very best. They should never allow themselves to say of any poor effort, whatever the haste or the weariness, "That will do."

Nothing else is so enervating as the indolent, self-indulgent spirit. He who thus seeks to save himself, loses himself. Youth should scorn self-indulgence in every form. It should court hardship rather than ease. What right have strong young men to demand luxury,—soft beds, smooth roads, light burdens, short hours? Rather it should be their pride to grapple with hardness and difficulty, and to be heroic in their struggles. Young men should be ashamed to do any duty indolently, or even to fall short of the best.

It is a great thing to have a lofty ideal and to live up to it. Michael Angelo said, "Nothing makes the soul so pure, so religious, as the endeavor to create something perfect; for God is perfect, and whoever strives for perfection strives for something Godlike." The blessing is in the striving.

"Not failure, but low aim, is crime."

Though we fail to reach our ideal, the effort to reach it does us good. First, it proves our faithfulness. How can we ever look God in the face, if we have not earnestly tried to do our best? But when we have struggled with all our might toward the attainment of the noble ideal which haunts us, though we have come short of it, we shall not be ashamed to stand before God at last, conscious that we have done our best.

Striving always after the perfect ideal also

lifts us step by step toward the ever-unattained excellence. We grow better through every effort we make to be better. Every time we try to do any most common work perfectly, we are doing also another work of far greater importance on our own character. The carpenter is a better man for having wrought a good piece of carpentering. The housekeeper is a better woman for having made her home beautiful, and filled it with comfort and the sweetness of love. Doing the most common tasks well makes the life itself nobler and more Christlike.

On the other hand, he who does anything indolently, in slovenly fashion, less skilfully than he could have done it, has not only left a piece of work in the world which will shame him some day, but has also done harm to his own soul.

We do not think enough of this effect on our character of what we do in our ordinary tasks. We say it makes no difference if we skimp our work when there is nothing important in it. You write a postal-card carelessly. The carpenter does not take pains with the piece of carpentering he is doing. The pupil does not get the lesson thoroughly. The housekeeper does not sweep the dark corners of her rooms. The author writes his book hurriedly, not doing his best. Neither of these persons thinks of any other evil result but that which is left in the work itself ; that they confess is not what it might have been. But in each case a far more serious evil result was left in the life of him who did his task in a negligent way. We are working all the while in two spheres, — on matter, where men see the kind of work we do, and on our own inner life, where only God's eye can see the marks we make.

We are not accustomed to consider this close identifying of our common task-work in the world with our own spiritual up-building. Carelessness in our daily duties hinders our growth and sanctification. Doing the best we can in our secular occupations makes us holier, and helps to fashion the image of Christ in our heart.

Thus it is much more important than we are apt to think that we strive always to do perfect work, even in the lowliest and the commonest things we undertake. What we do outside for men's eyes, we do also within for God's eyes. Slovenly work in school or in business or on a building or on a farm or in the home is also slovenly work on one's own character.

Many catastrophes come in later years from doing imperfect or careless work in youth. When digging for the foundation of a great building, the workmen came upon a piece of old wall. "That will do," they said; and they left it in the new wall, building round it. The great structure went up, and was filled with business. One day there was a crash. The fragment of old wall had given way, and the whole building fell in ruin.

Continually, young people are leaving in the foundation walls of their character a fault, a wrong habit, a weakness, a flaw. It would be hard to dig it out. It is easier just to build over and around it, and so they let it stay. "That will do," they say apologetically. Then years afterward, in some great stress or strain, the character fails and falls into ruin; it is seen then that that careless piece of foundation-building was the cause of it all.

No more serious problem arises in a young person's life than the temptation, ever-recurring, to do things negligently, to pass slipshod or slovenly work. Nothing but the best we can do in the circumstances should ever be allowed to leave our hands. Never should any young person permit his work, his words, his life, any of his habits, to be ruled by a motto so unworthy, so debasing in its influence, as, "That will do."

CHAPTER XXI.

A HIGH SENSE OF HONOR.

EVERYTHING that is beautiful in life should be most earnestly coveted by every young person. Youth is the time for the building of character. What we expect to be when we are out in the world in mid-life, we must begin to be when we are in school. If we would have a good name at forty, we must do only worthy and honorable things through the years that lead to forty.

Nothing is too small to take into the account in the making up of life. We may say there is no harm in this, that that is not wrong, that we would be foolish to care for such little things as moralists insist upon. But "trifles make perfection." It is ofttimes the little blemishes that mar the beauty, the little "no harms" that dim the lustre, of the character. "Dead flies cause the ointment of the perfumer to send forth a stinking savor."

There are many little things which seem not to be sinful, not distinctly immoral, which yet indicate a low moral tone. It is very easy to grow lenient with one's self, to relax the severe demands of one's conscience, and to drop into little self-indulgences which not many years past one could not have been induced to admit into one's life.

Many men find themselves doing things in their mid-years which in their young manhood they could not have consented to do. There is need, therefore, for the cultivation among young people of a high sense of honor, and the maintenance of a lofty standard of life and conduct. There are many temptations to things which are not altogether honorable. Every such temptation should be met with resolute firmness. Only the sternest and most rigorous self-discipline will keep one's life up to a high standard in this regard. It is easy to think that what is conventional in conduct is good enough — being as good as other people are. But we must take no lower standard than absolute perfection. We must set our watches by the sun, not by any other person's watch.

A high sense of honor should make it impossible for one to do anything petty or small, to speak unkindly of a friend, or to repeat a confidential conversation or anything told in confidence.

This law of honor applies to all that one may

A HIGH SENSE OF HONOR. 155

learn of a family in which one has been a guest. There may have been little occurrences in the household life which it would be easy to gossip about outside. Sometimes even in excellent homes there are small infelicities at table, discussions which grow warm, differences of opinion about this or that. There may be family peculiarities, or little habits which seem strange. No one can be a guest for a few days in any home without seeing or hearing something which it would be easy to talk about and criticise. But this is a case in which a sense of honor forbids any mention outside of what one may have heard or seen. A guest in a home is received in confidence; and the acceptance of the hospitality seals one's lips and forbids any comment or criticism, or the rehearsal of anything that would in the slightest way reflect on the character of the home or the home-life.

There are many other applications of this principle. Too often there is a lack of highest honor in friendship. There are many who are not careful in speaking of their friends in their absence, who join too readily in criticism of them, when a fine sense of honor would lead them to speak words of defence. There is no truer test of friendship than the way one speaks of another behind the other's back.

Another mark of honor in friendship is loyalty when it costs something to be loyal. Our friend is in need of help, which we can give, but only at much personal sacrifice. True love always serves. God so loved that he gave. Love always gives, and the giving is the measure of the loving. Christ loved and served unto the uttermost. What we will do or suffer for one we love is the measure of our loving. Too many friendships are found wanting when there is need for deed as well as word.

A word may be said about honor in money matters. There are some good people who are very negligent in paying their debts. The borrowing propensity is too much indulged. They are always getting loans of little amounts from friends and neighbors. They want the money only until to-morrow; but they forget, or at least fail, to return it. Young people should resolutely determine that in all such matters they will maintain the highest honor. As far as possible they should "owe no man anything," keeping out of debt absolutely; but if they have occasion to ask a favor, they should repay it at the hour they promised to do it. In business a man's note going to protest hurts his commercial standing, perhaps leads to his downfall among men. When a man's word goes to protest, although it be only in a matter of five cents or a postage-stamp, harm has been done to his reputation.

There is need, too, for a fine sense of honor in the handling of the money which belongs to others. Almost every society has a treasurer — often a young person. The amount of money in hand may never be large; but the honor required in the treasurer is the same, however small the sum that is held in trust. Sometimes there is a temptation to use the money in one's own affairs, as there is no present need for it in the society, and will be no call for it for a time. There is not the slightest thought of appropriating the funds for any but temporary use; when the society needs them they will be paid out of one's own pocket. But there have been cases when the money thus used could not be returned when it was called for.

Sometimes, too, money held in the hands of a treasurer is allowed to pass out to help a friend, another member of the family perhaps, with the assurance that when it is required it will be returned. There have been cases of this kind in which serious trouble has occurred because the money could not be refunded.

But whether there is trouble or not, the question of honor remains unchanged. We have no right ever to borrow or to lend from trust funds in our hands for any purpose whatever. Such funds are sacred, and should be kept inviolable.

Thus in every department of life we should set as our standard the highest sense of honor in all our conduct, and in all our relations to others. God desires truth in the inward parts, and that truth should show itself without blemish or spot in every word and act.

It was said of Sir Isaac Newton, by those who knew him most intimately, that he had the whitest soul they had ever known. His heart was set ever upon finding out and telling others the simple, honest, straightforward truth about any subject with which he had to do. No selfish thought, no hidden motive, came in to lead him to vary in the smallest particular from the truth. His motto always was, "Let me know and say what is true." Those who live thus will honor God, will win for themselves an honored reputation, and will bless the world.

CHAPTER XXII.

ON DOING OUR BEST.

YOUR best is all you are ever required to do; indeed, no one can do more. It is not some other one's best that is expected of you, either, but your own. Sometimes people forget this, and worry because they cannot do as well as some other person does. Our gifts differ: no two are just alike in their capacity. Besides, no two are ever at precisely the same point in their progress. Of a student in a lower form it is not demanded that he do as well as one in a higher class. The young girl who has been taking music-lessons only a year is not expected to play as well as her sister who has been studying for five or six years with the best teachers. You are to do your own best, not some other one's.

It is a shame for any one ever to do less than his best. It may be only the writing of a postal-card, but it should be done as carefully and neatly as you can possibly do it. You should never send a carelessly written scrawl to any one for a letter. Some persons fall into wretched habits of writing. Their chirography is execrable, so illegible that their letters can be deciphered only by the most painful effort, and then ofttimes only half made out. Some people seem to fancy that plain, beautiful handwriting is a mark of inferiority of some kind; at least, it is a common tradition that all great men write very illegibly. But, really, bad handwriting is never a mark of genius. No doubt some great men have written miserably enough, but their bad chirography was no proof of their greatness. Nor does it follow that scrawling, unreadable handwriting will make you great. Write as plainly and beautifully as you can. Think of the person who is to read your letter, and have pity. Many eyes are strained and hurt in deciphering careless writing, to say nothing of the straining of patience and the hurting of the temper caused by the trying ordeal.

The same motto — always do your best — should be applied to everything we do. A man who had risen from a very humble beginning to distinction, even to great eminence, when asked the secret of his successful life, said he had always sought to do his best in whatever he undertook, summoning the best thought, the finest skill, the greatest energy, of which he was capable, to every piece of work he was doing.

He demanded of himself, too, that to-day's best should always be better than yesterday's.

It were well for us if we all would make and follow inflexibly such a rule as this. No most trivial thing should we ever do carelessly. All work is for God, and it is sacrilege to do anything for him in a slovenly, negligent manner. It is a desecration to put marred or careless work on any block we carve for God's temple. The workmen on the old cathedrals wrought as conscientiously and as perfectly on the parts of the building which would be high up, far out of human sight, as on the altar-rail or the carvings of the great doors which every eye should see and admire.

When a heathen artist was asked why he took so much pains with the back of the figures he was chiselling, since they would be against the walls and no one would ever see them, his noble answer was, "The gods will see them." Always we are working for God's eye, and should ever do our best.

Not only are we working for God's eye, but it is God's own work that we are doing. Whether a man is a carpenter, a painter, a stone-cutter, a farmer, a teacher, or a minister, it is God's work he has in hand; and he must do his best. Old Stradivarius, the violin-maker, was right when he said that if his hand slacked he would rob God. We rob God whenever we do anything carelessly, or do less than our best. A writer says, "The universe is not quite complete without my work well done." We misrepresent God and disappoint him when we do in a slovenly way anything, however small, that he gives us to do.

The lesson is for the housekeeper, for the student, for the teacher, for the preacher, for the boy at play, for the singer — less than the best we can do dishonors God. Get your lessons at school as well as you can. In the games in which you take a part, do not play languidly, indifferently, indolently, but with enthusiasm and earnestness, and all the skill you can command. Dress neatly and tidily as you can; even if your clothes are well worn, have them clean. Make your room as bright and beautiful as possible. Always speak as correctly, gracefully, and impressively as you can, enunciating every syllable distinctly, and making sure of your pronunciation.

We may carry the lesson also into the highest things. We should live our best every day. We should always "approve the things that are excellent." We should be just as careful when no human eye is upon us as when we are working under the gaze of thousands. God is not a hard master, not unreasonable in his demands upon us. He does not expect great skill in a beginner. He does not demand that a child-Christian shall be as mature in thought, disposition, act, and character as an aged saint. He does not expect a plain Christian to be as eloquent in witnessing for Christ as the minister, after years of training and experience. But he expects us to do always what we can, — our best.

"She hath done what she could" was very sweet and gracious commendation. But Mary's "what she could" was a rich offering; it was the costliest thing in her possession. We must never put God off with anything unworthy. In ancient times no lame or blemished animal could be offered in sacrifice to God; the offerer must always bring the best he had. We should never give God anything broken or soiled. It seems desecration to put in God's offering torn bills and battered coins, or to give in charity garments which are so worn that we ourselves would be ashamed to wear them. We should give God the best of everything we have, — the true first-fruits of all our life and work.

We should make the most we can of our life, and rise to better attainments every day. The way to do this is in every smallest task and duty, in every thought, word, and act, to do our very best. Lowell puts it well in his lines "For an Autograph," when he tells us that though the thought may be old and ofttimes expressed, it is his at last who says it best : —

> Life is a leaf of paper white,
> Whereon each one of us may write
> His word or two, and then comes night.
>
> "Lo, time and space enough," we cry,
> "To write an epic!" so we try
> Our nibs upon the edge, and die.
>
> Muse not which way the pen to hold,
> Luck hates the slow and loves the bold,
> Soon comes the darkness and the cold.
>
> Greatly begin! though thou have time
> But for a line, be that sublime;
> Not failure, but low aim, is crime.
>
> Ah! with what lofty hope we came!
> But we forget it, dream of fame,
> And scrawl, as I do here, a name.

CHAPTER XXIII.

ABOUT YOUR SHADOW.

THERE is in the New Testament a beautiful story which tells of the power of a good man's shadow. The people brought out their sick, and laid them along the sides of the road when this man was to pass, that his shadow might fall upon them; and we are told that they were healed, every one.

Of course it was a supernatural power which wrought so wondrously in that man's shadow. God was pleased to use it in this way to impress the people with the divineness of Christianity. We cannot expect that we shall be able to work miracles of healing through our shadow. But we all cast shadows wherever we go, and our shadow has either wholesome or unwholesome influence over other lives.

We think of a shadow as something dark. It is made by an object coming between us and the light. It is therefore an intercepting, a cutting off, of brightness. Night is a shadow, —the shadow made by the earth coming between us and the sun. It is not an altogether unwelcome phenomenon, however, though the sun is hidden for a time and darkness gathers about us. Even night has its compensations. One is the glorious revealing of the stars, which we should never see but for our passing into the shadow of the night. There are other shadows which in like manner reveal more than they hide. There are sorrows which darken the world for us, but show us meanwhile the stars of divine promise.

Every one who approaches us or stands by us casts a shadow upon us. There are some human shadows which make the world darker for us. There are people whose presence does not bring light and joy to us. They make us less happy. They make it harder for us to live sweetly, cheerfully, and victoriously. They come in with their sadness, their fears, their worries, their doubts, and cast deep gloom over us.

There are other persons whose shadow is white. Instead of intercepting the light, the brightness appears to stream through them and to be all the brighter. The rainbow is a kind of glorified shadow. A sunbeam falls upon a drop of water, and its wonderful threads are unravelled, disentangled, as it shines through, and instead of a white shadow we have seven colors spread upon the cloud. There are some people who act on the light of Christ's love as the crystal drop of water acts upon the beam of sunshine, separating it into elements of wonderful beauty, interpreting it into the loveliness of human tenderness, sympathy, and helpfulness, and bringing it down into the sphere of common life.

Every Christian should cast a rainbow shadow, not cutting off from friends the brightness of the light of Christ's face, but making it all the richer because of its human interpreting. The blessing of the love of Christ should be in the influence of every Christian. Wherever we go there should be healing in our shadow. Others should be better and truer for seeing and knowing us. Wherever we go we should carry cheer and gladness. It should be easier for our friends to be good because they know us and see our life. Our shadow, even as we pass along the street, should heal those upon whom it falls. We should always be inspirers of the good possibilities in those whom we influence.

> "Be noble, and the nobleness that lies
> In other men, sleeping, but never dead,
> Will rise in majesty to meet thine own."

This subject is a very personal one, for every one has a shadow of his own. The question is, What kind of shadow do you cast? What is the effect of your presence on other people? Do you inspire cheerfulness, gladness, and hope wherever you go? Or is the effect of your influence depressing and disheartening?

There are persons who suppose themselves to be very sympathetic with others in trouble who really make trouble and pain harder to bear, or, rather, make their friends less able to endure. When they sit down beside the sick, the whole drift of their words is towards the emphasizing and intensifying of the illness. They draw out from the patient a recital of his sufferings and of his own feelings, and by look and word express their sense of the seriousness of his condition. But they do nothing to put new strength or cheer into his heart. They think they have been playing the part of a very gentle and sympathetic friend, whereas they have only aggravated the illness, and made it harder for the patient to endure. They only deepen life's shadows for others.

When they find a man discouraged over any unfortunate circumstances in his life, they listen to his plaint with tender feelings, expressing their pity, assenting to all that he says about his difficulties or misfortunes, but not saying one heartening word.

They come to a friend who is in sorrow, and sit down beside him in his darkened home, weeping with him, and entering into all the painful elements of his grief; but they fail to bring to him any strong comfort. They make it only harder for him to endure his sorrow.

In each case these good people think they have shown deep and tender sympathy because they have condoled with their friends in their trouble. But in each case they have left a depressing influence. They have entered fully enough into the painful elements of the experience which they wished to alleviate; but there is no help in this, if that be all that one does. Such sympathy is hurtful. It only makes the burden heavier and the way darker, while the heart is left with less hope and comfort for its struggle. There are too many people that cast such shadows as these. They intercept the light, and leave darkness and chill on the life on which their influence falls.

Peter's shadow had healing power in it. The sick upon whom it rested even for a moment, as he passed by, became strong and well, and rose up cured and happy. There are those in every community who carry with them, wherever they go, a like influence of healing and blessing. They bear into a sick-room a delicate sympathy, which not only enters into the experience of the suffering, but puts new cheer and hope into the heart of the sufferer. They speak encouraging and inspiring words. Their face has in it a message of cheer wherever it appears. They bring some promise of God, some word of hope and encouragement. The discouraged man they meet is made to feel not only that he has found a friend who is truly interested in him, but also that, after all, his case is not so hopeless as he imagined it to be, and that he need not despair. He is ready to try again. The mourner whom they visit is made conscious of a friendship that not only understands his sorrow and is truly sympathetic, but that also puts into his heart a secret strength, which, though it does not take away any part of his grief, yet leaves him better able to bear it.

These are illustrations of the power of a healing shadow. There are people who carry benedictions wherever they go. Every life they overshadow, even for a moment, receives some blessing from them. The secret is that they are filled with love — the love of Christ abiding in them. Love is always self-forgetful, and desires to do good to others; to minister, not to be ministered unto; to help, not to be helped. Love is thoughtful also; careful never to give pain, to add to another's burdens, to make life harder for another.

Another element in a healthful and health-giving shadow is victoriousness. We must be overcomers ourselves before we can help others to overcome. One who himself yields to discouragement cannot be an encourager of others. One who is crushed by sorrow, and does not get God's comfort for himself, cannot be a comforter of others in their sorrow. It is frequently said that one who has suffered is fitted to be a helper of others because he understands what pain and struggle are, and knows how to help. But this depends on how he has come through his suffering or his trial. If he has not been victorious, if he lies still in the shadows of defeat, he has no experience that fits him to enter into helpful sympathy with others in like experiences. But one who has been a victor in life's battles is able to be a comforter, and an inspirer of those he meets who are in the midst of struggle or trial. If you would have a healing shadow, you must learn the secret of Christ's victoriousness.

Every young person should seek to have an

influence which will be a benediction wherever it reaches. The way to have such a shadow is to be filled with the mind that was in Christ Jesus. Then our name will be as ointment poured forth — a holy fragrance. Then our life will be full of wholesome and healthful inspirations. Then wherever we go we will make it easier for others to live victoriously. Some one makes this little prayer: —

> May every soul that touches mine,
> Be it the slightest contact, get therefrom some good,
> Some little grace, one kindly thought,
> One aspiration yet unfelt, one bit of courage.

The other day one who is ill wrote to a friend: "You are such a comfort. You make people forget half their pain when you are near them." This friend has learned the secret of the healing shadow.

CHAPTER XXIV.

YOUR LITTLE BROTHER.

MANY young people have younger brothers, little brothers sometimes, in their home. In every such case there is a responsibility which is not always recognized. If older brothers and sisters knew the influence they have over their little brothers it would make them very thoughtful. It was a belief of the Jews that to every person was assigned a guardian angel, who watched all the steps from birth to death. Perhaps this is true. It certainly is a very comforting thought. But whether it be true or not that particular angels are assigned to care for people's lives in their journey through this world, it is no doubt true that older brothers and sisters are divinely appointed guardians for younger children. An angel is a messenger. No doubt many of God's angels are human friends whom he sends on his errands. Mrs. Sangster has some pleasant lines about angels. She refers to the appearance of these messengers in the olden days, and then says: —

But in these days I know my angels well;
   They brush my garments on the common way;
They take my hand, and very softly tell
   Some bit of comfort in the waning day.

And though their angel names I do not ken,
   Though in their faces human want I read;
They are God-given to this world of men,
   God-sent to bless it in its hour of need.

Child, mother, dearest wife, brave hearts that take
   The rough and bitter cross, and help us bear
Its heavy weight when strength is like to break;
   God bless you each, our angels unaware.

The story of Miriam and little Moses is one of the most charming stories of the Bible. While the baby lay in the ark among the bulrushes, by the water's edge, the young girl with quick ear and keen eye stood not far away, — near enough to see all that went on, and to be of instant help in case of danger. In many and many a home older sisters have played the *rôle* of Miriam to perfection. Many a man to-day occupying an important position in the world owes the opportunities by which he was enabled to rise to his position to an older sister, who kept sacred watch over his infancy and early years. There are many men to-day in the professions and occupying high places in the world, who came from homes amid straitened circumstances, and who owe all they are to the sister who forgot herself, practised self-denials, and toiled early and late, that the brother she loved might go to school and to college, and thus have a chance to rise to the honor which she in her loving heart had dreamed for him.

Then sometimes alas! when the man is out in the world, wearing honors, he forgets the weary woman, living somewhere in obscurity, perhaps in poverty, to whom he owes all his distinction and greatness.

It may be worth while to call the attention of older brothers and sisters to the little brother at home, who needs guidance, encouragement, and stimulus. Far more than you know he watches you, and is influenced by your every movement. He will be impressed much more also by what you do and what you are than by any teaching he may receive.

It is important that you know just how to make the most of your influence over him. You cannot do it by perpetually nagging at him; nagging is one of the most mischievous vices of the home-life. It is all the worse because it is practised in the name of piety and virtue. The best you can do for him is first of all to be good yourself. When the young Princess Victoria discovered one day that she was near the throne, she said, "I must be good." The thought of the great responsibility which some day might be hers impressed her most wholesomely. When you think of the influence you are to exercise over your little brother, you should settle it once for all that you will be good.

Another thing you can do will be to form a close friendship with him. Take him into your confidence. Let him talk to you freely and familiarly.

Teach him to trust you, and never betray his confidence. Be a loyal friend to him. Treat even his most childish fancies with respect. Never laugh at him. Do not hurry his development: it is like trying to hasten the opening of a flower; only harm can be done by such a process.

You can answer his questions, and you ought to do it very patiently. Remember it is a new world in which he is living. Every-day brings him into a new chamber of wonders. He ought to ask questions. He would not be a wholesome child if he did not. You can help him by trying to answer these questions. You can guide his reading. You can quietly influence him in the choosing of his friends. This is very important. He does not know the good from the evil, and you can withdraw him from the company of those with whom it were better he should not associate. You can set before him visions of beauty which will become influences to draw him toward the best things.

If your own heart be right, and if you keep yourself in the spirit of childhood, you will be able to lead him in safe ways. The world is full of dangers. Your little brother hears on the streets many things he ought not to hear. You can quietly lead him so that he will instinctively repel all temptations to anything low or base or mean or impure. You can turn his mind toward the possibilities of beauty within his reach.

Without forcing him into precocity, which is monstrosity, you can continually keep before him noble things in disposition, in conduct, in character, thus quietly inspiring in him the desire to fill his own life with such worthy things.

There is a great responsibility in having a little brother. He is always around, and you cannot get out of his sight. He has keen eyes too, and sees all that you do. You dare not live carelessly in his presence, for you may become his stumbling-block. There should be nothing in your example which you would be sorry to see again in him.

This little brother of yours loves you, and wants to trust you. Your influence over him will be almost unbounded; you must see to it that this influence is pure and wholesome in every way.

The older brother must answer for his little brother; he is his keeper. He must make himself worthy of his sacred trust. If his own heart is not clean, if his own mind is not wholesome, if his own hands are stained, he is not fit to be a boy's older brother.

The thing for the older brother to do in such a case is not to thrust the boy away from his natural place of confidence and affection, but to bring up his own life to the true standard of purity, sweetness, and beauty, where he shall be worthy to be a friend of Christ's little ones.

CHAPTER XXV.

THE BLESSING OF WORK.

SOME persons have the impression that work is part of the curse that sin brought into the world. They imagine that if our first parents had not fallen, they would never have had anything to do, that they would have walked about forever among the trees of Paradise and by the rivers, having a good time. They suppose that they were doomed to work as part of the penalty of their sin.

But this is a mistaken impression, which a careful reading of the story of Eden and the fall will quickly remove. We learn here that after the creation the Lord took the man, and put him in the garden of Eden to "dress it and to keep it." That is, work was part of the unfallen life in Paradise. It was never meant that man should have nothing to do. Idleness was not part of the Edenic happiness.

No doubt the fall changed the character of work. Man was turned out of the garden; and these words were spoken to him, "Cursed is the ground for thy sake; in toil shalt thou eat of it all the days of thy life; thorns also and thistles shall it bring forth to thee; and thou shalt eat the herb of the field; in the sweat of thy face shalt thou eat bread, till thou return unto the ground."

We may infer that before the fall work was congenial and pleasant, without burden or care, and that after sin had left its blight on the earth work became toil, with vexing and sorrow, with thorns and thistles for yield instead of golden harvests. Yet we must never forget that work was part of man's lot, even in Paradise. Therefore work itself is not a curse, but a blessing. All life testifies to this. Everywhere we find work one of the conditions of good and happiness. God himself is active. "My Father worketh hitherto, and I work," said the Master. God is never idle. The Decalogue enjoins work as a divine ordinance. "Six days shalt thou labor."

Jesus sanctified labor by working with his own hands as a carpenter. St. Paul wrought at a common trade while engaged in doing some of the most wonderful missionary work the world has ever known. He was never ashamed of being a workingman, but gloried in the fact that his own hands had ministered to his neces-

THE BLESSING OF WORK. 181

sities. He also spoke strongly in commendation of work, and stingingly of the reproach of idleness. "If any will not work, neither let him eat." Then he added that he had heard of some that walked among the Christians disorderly, that worked not at all, but were busybodies. That is, being idle, with nothing to do, they busied themselves in other people's affairs, not helping them, but meddling, gossipping. This is one of the surest fruits of idleness. These persons the apostle commanded and exhorted that they should work quietly, and eat their own bread, — bread earned with their own hands.

It would be easy to gather from the pens of many writers strong words on the blessing of work. For example, this from Emerson: "Work in every hour, paid or unpaid; see only that thou work, and thou canst not escape the reward; whether thy work be fine or coarse, planting corn or writing epics, so only it be honest work, done to thine own approbation, it shall earn a reward to the senses as well as to the thought. No matter how often defeated, you are born to victory. The reward of a thing well done is to have done it."

Henry Drummond said: "The three ingredients of a perfect life are — work, which gives opportunity; God, who gives happiness; love, that gives warmth. Whenever the world is all wrong, seemingly, examine your life, and see if one of these ingredients is not wanting. The ideal perfect and divine life was spent, not with a book, but with a hammer and a saw. There is nothing greater in the world than the simple doing of every-day tasks. Work is our moral education; no work, no opportunities. The farm is not a place only for the growing of stock; the shop is not the place for the growing of machines alone. They are the places for the growing of souls."

Work is one of the best means of grace. Whatever helps in one's growth and development of life and character is a means of grace. Without work one never can grow. Idleness breeds disease. It is always unwholesome. No matter how much money one may have, though it be unnecessary for him to earn anything, yet for the sake of the saving of his own life and for his mere physical well-being, he ought to do his share in the world's work. We have no right to our daily bread until we have earned it. We must work, too, for the sake of others. Not to do anything is to be a parasite, giving nothing to the world, which gives us so many blessings.

One cannot be a good Christian and be idle, unless one is really physically disqualified for labor of every kind; in such a case the blessing comes upon the willing heart, though the hands must be folded. Prayer without work is but one wing to the soul, which can only flutter along the ground and cannot fly. There are times when even holy devotions must be given up for holier duty. Among the legends of the monastic orders it is written: " Although St. Francesca was unwearied in her devotions, yet if during her prayers she was called away by her husband or any domestic duty, she would close the book cheerfully, saying that a wife and mother when called upon must quit her God at the altar to find him in her domestic affairs." This is very suggestive. There are times when to stay on one's knees at prayer would be sin : God calls to some imperative service, and his call must be obeyed.

When we pray that grace may abound in us, and that we may become more and more like Christ, the blessing will not likely come in frames of mind, in devout feelings, in exalted spiritual states, but in new calls to duty, to service, to work, —

> " Till there seems room for everything but Thee,
> And never time for anything but these."

It is in our work that God comes nearest to us, and that Christ enters most deeply into our experiences, and brings to us the sweetest joy.

"The busy fingers fly, the eyes may see
    Only the glancing needle which they hold;
But all my life is blossoming inwardly,
And every breath is like a litany,
    While through each labor, like a thread of gold,
Is woven the sweet consciousness of thee."

The kind of work we should do depends upon what we are divinely fitted to do. It may be on a farm, or in a shop, or in a store. It may be in common household tasks. It may be in some intellectual pursuit, or in direct service for Christ. Every one should have a calling, and should devote himself to it with enthusiasm. A large part of the blessing is in the work itself. Even if the thing we do is not valuable, or seems to yield no result, there is still a blessing in merely being busy. If one has to work without pay, it is better than to be idle. If one has nothing to do, it is better to find some task, though it be but carrying water to pour into the sand, than to sit with folded hands in unwholesome idleness.

The lesson is for the young people, because it is in youth that we must learn to work if ever we do. Work is health. Work is life. Work is the way to strength and power. Work builds up the character, and knits the thews of manliness. Work carries in itself one of the prime secrets of happiness. Idleness is never truly happy; but he who labors with all his might has a good conscience, and sleeps sweetly. Work is one of God's best ways of giving comfort. "Had it not been for my work," said one after a great sorrow, "I should never have rallied; my hard work saved me."

These are suggestions of the blessings of work. The young people are fortunate who by the conditions of their early life are required to engage in regular, uninterrupted, and even severe labor. Thus they are not only trained to self-dependence, but their abilities are developed, their character is formed into strength; they are prepared for happy, wholesome, useful living, and their lives thus become blessings in the world.

CHAPTER XXVI.

A GIRL'S QUESTIONS.

EVERY girl has questions. Her brain teems with them — her heart too. She ought to have questions. If she had not she would not be a living girl, at least she would be living to very small purpose. Questions are the keys which open doors within which we find life's better things.

Girls are not all alike. It would not be true to say that to answer one girl's questions would be to answer every girl's questions. But certainly to answer one girl's questions will throw light upon the questions of many others. From a bright, interesting letter, bristling with interrogation points, a little handful of earnest inquiries is gathered for this chapter, in the belief that others may be helped by the answers that are given.

"There is one thing — we hear it talked about so much, and even preached about — how girls fall below what is expected of them, and are such disappointments." The writer continues, "What really is expected of girls? It hardly seems fair for people to make out their own ideal, and then measure all girls by that one standard. Aren't circumstances to make any difference, and different natures, surroundings, and friends? There are so many things which ought to count. It does seem as though people sometimes uncharitably forget the 'Judge not.'"

That is a fair question, — "What is expected of girls?" No doubt there is much thoughtless unreasonableness in some of these expectations. Really nothing should be expected of girls but that they be true and noble, living near Christ, and faithfully realizing the religion of the cross. Of course it is very unfair to expect all girls, or even any two of them, to be precisely alike. It is said that no two faces in all the world's millions are alike in every feature. Much less can any two lives be exactly the same. Nothing hurts one more than trying to be like somebody else. Let every girl be her sweetest and best self, growing into the beauty of her noble ideals. Let her please God with her life — that is all.

"When a girl wakes up to the knowledge that she is disagreeable, — a fact that other people have found out long ago, — what shall she do?"

It surely is not a pleasant waking for any girl, thus to become conscious some sad day that she is disagreeable. It is apt to discourage her, and to make the disagreeableness even more marked and emphatic. But the question is, "What shall she do?" People answer, "Make yourself attractive; be agreeable; be lovable." But it is not easy to follow such advice. One cannot, just in a moment, by a sudden resolve, work such a transformation in one's self. A girl who is not beautiful cannot by a mental process make herself lovely. One who has an unhappy disposition cannot by merely willing it become sunny and cheerful. One whose manners are disagreeable cannot some morning in her room lay off all that is offensive, unattractive, or unrefined in herself, and come out into the street with graceful and winning ways. Such transformations can be wrought only gradually. The beautiful things are set in lessons for us, line upon line, and are to be learned, wrought into the character little by little. The unattractive girl can make herself attractive, but not by any mere resolve to be so. Magical transformations belong only to fairy stories, not to real life.

The only cure for any kind of disagreeableness is love in the heart. Mr. Drummond tells of a plain young girl who grew into wonderful sweetness of disposition; and the secret was found at last in a little word of Scripture which was the real creed of her life, — "Whom having not seen, ye love." The love of Christ in her heart had transformed her. We know, too, how it transformed Mary; sitting at the feet of Jesus, and hearing his words, love for him changed her into radiant beauty.

It is the want of love that ails all disagreeable people; they do not love, and they are not lovable. They are selfish or they are censorious, or they are discontented and fretful, or they are proud, haughty, and supercilious, or they are exacting or soured, or they are self-conscious and unwholesome in their life. Love will cure it, however, whatever the disagreeableness is. It will make the homely face beautiful. People forget unattractive ways if the heart and life be sweet with love. Some one tells of a homely woman who became the best loved and the most honored woman in all the community simply by a life of love which wrought itself out in her in untiring service. The only thing for the disagreeable girl to do is to get her heart and life full of love.

"Then there are the blue times — I wish I knew how to keep out of the blues."

The dictionary defines "blues" as low spirits, melancholy, hypochondria. The word is said to be a contraction for blue-devils, which is a suggestion of delirium, when evil spirits seem to have possession. This somewhat uncanny suggestion ought to warn every girl against ever yielding to the blues. It is letting into her life an evil influence, an evil spirit, which can produce only wretchedness.

But how to keep from having the blues, or how to get clear of them, is the question. One way is to train one's self ever to look on the bright side, and never on the dark. The secret of this habit must be found in two things, — faithful obedience to God, and simple trust in God. The peace of God in the heart will always drive out the blues. There is an inspired word which says, "Thou wilt keep him in perfect peace whose mind is stayed on thee." Here we have the secret of peace, — staying the mind upon God. The keeping us in peace belongs, then, to God. One who is thus kept cannot be blue.

But suppose one has allowed the blues to come without resistance into the heart again and again, till now one seems to have no power to combat the miserable feeling; is there any cure? Yes, although it will take longer time to dislodge the demon, and the dislodging will be harder to accomplish. Jesus said there were certain demons which could be driven out only by special prayer and fasting. He meant they were very hard to cast out. When the blues have had their way in a life for a long time it takes much prayer and sore struggle to drive the demons out. Still, no case is hopeless when we have Christ. The worst depression of spirits can be transformed into the joy of the Lord in the heart. Jesus overcame all the world; and there is no evil so strong that he cannot subdue it, and put in its place a virtue.

"Then, how about the people you don't like? Miss R——, for example? I don't want to draw into my shell, and be cold and disagreeable to her, and yet— I know she is lonely and homesick, and she asked me to love her if I could. But if you knew how she rubs me the wrong way, you would understand. What do you do with such people? Or perhaps it is, What do you do with yourself?"

The last question puts the emphasis where it will have to be kept, — "What do you do with yourself?" When other people are disagreeable or hateful, when they antagonize us and irritate us, — rub us the wrong way, — it is not likely that we can do much to change them, to make them sweet and agreeable, to incline them to be more kindly, respectful, genial, or affectionate toward us. We shall have to school ourselves into greater patience, into firmer self-restraint, into sweeter humility, into gentler love, so that the disagreeableness and the unkindliness of others shall have no power to disturb the holy quiet of our soul.

The real problem in life is not to find easy circumstances in which to live, — a new paradise where nothing uncongenial shall ever come near to us, — but to have in ourselves the secret of sweetness, which nothing can disturb. We are so to relate ourselves to others that their evil shall have no power to hurt us. We may not be able to transform into lovableness the people we do not like; but instead of drawing into our shell, and being cold and disagreeable to them, our heart must go out to them in love, and we must be as Christ to them. That is the best way to cure them. Besides, when we begin to treat them in this way, we shall find in them beauty and good we had never suspected before. The way to bring out the best there is in others is to expect the best, and to treat them always with love. Loving people hides their faults, and calls out in them whatsoever things are true, whatsoever things are lovely.

These are some of the questions of one girl. Her closing sentences are: " Don't forget the encouraging part. If people only knew how we long for it sometimes! A little praise occasionally would not make us vain, would not turn our head, and certainly would do us more good than harm. It would help us sometimes so much!"

This is very true. People need nothing so much as encouragement. An artist said his mother's kiss made him a painter. Wise cheer is always full of inspiration. The man who writes or speaks discouraging words is a doer of evil. We have no right ever to be discouragers; we should live always to be encouragers.

In every girl's heart visions of beauty throng, and every one of these visions is a glimpse of something she may become. Her mission is to get these holy visions wrought into her life and character.

CHAPTER XXVII.

WHAT IS THE COMFORT?

He had just completed his long course of preparation. He had been graduated from the University, and then from the Theological Seminary. He had been called as pastor of an interesting church, and had been ordained and installed. Then almost immediately he became ill. He was tenderly watched over. The best medical skill was procured in his behalf, and all that could be done was done. But all availed not. One October day he sank away into the quietness and stillness of death.

Truly it seemed a mysterious providence. The sadness is always peculiar when a young person dies. The old have filled up the measure of their days, and have finished their work; but the young are only beginning to realize the dream of their heart. This young man died at the close of a long and costly preparation for life. He gave also unusual promise of a most successful career. "He will be an eloquent preacher," men said. Yet after all this course of training, and with all this brilliant promise for the future, he had no opportunity to try his powers. The consecrated talents laid upon the altar were employed in no active service of earth. Ready for beautiful and noble work, his hands were at once folded in death's repose.

From childhood his parents had watched over his life with gentlest care. They had brought him up for Christ. They had given the most diligent and intelligent thought to his education, sparing no pains and no cost that he might be well fitted for the chosen work of his life. They had dreamed large things for his future. They had expected that his voice would be heard throughout the land in eloquent tones as he delivered his message from God to men. No words can describe the bitterness of their grief and disappointment as they bent over the coffin, which held not only the precious form of their beloved son, but seemed to hold also all the fond dreams and hopes of their hearts for him.

What is the comfort of the religion of Christ in such a case as this? There must be comfort, for life has no experiences for the believer in which the light of the gospel does not shine. One comfort is that death really interrupts nothing beautiful and good in a Christian life.

A mother was speaking of a daughter who had died just after finishing a long course of education, and was lamenting that all her costly training had been in vain. The friend to whom she was speaking replied that all education was valueless which was not for eternity.

It might seem that it was scarcely worth while to spend so much in the education of this young man, when he did not live to make any use of his trained powers in this world. But we must remember that his life belonged to Christ, and that his early death meant only that his Master had called him to service elsewhere, nearer the throne. His parents did not know it; but through all the years of their self-denial for his sake and their patient nurturing of his life, they were educating and preparing their son for service in the blessed fields of glory, instead of for ministry on the earth. Could any honor be greater than this? The long, patient training was not in vain; he is finding opportunities now for the use of all his fine gifts and cultured powers in the holy service in which he is engaged close to Christ.

There was another most pathetic element in this providential mystery. The young man was engaged to a noble girl. For years they had loved each other, and had ardently dreamed of the day when they would be united in marriage. This dream, too, seemed on the verge of fulfilment. They intended in a little while to be wedded, and then to set up their home in the parish over which he had become the pastor. But this sweet dream was not realized; it, too, lay among the broken hopes that were folded up and shut away in the coffin.

What comfort has the gospel of Christ for this sorely bereft and sorrowing child in her pathetic loneliness? For one thing, she has the assurance that this strange thing which has happened was no accident. The two faithful lovers had their sweet dream of life together in this world. They hoped to share each other's cares and trials, and to go hand in hand in their work for Christ. But this was not the divine purpose for their lives. From the beginning it was the Master's plan that one of them, when fully trained and ready for service, should be transferred to another field, in a brighter country, while the other should remain on earth, to serve Christ here, without the loved companionship.

This separation, therefore, was no accident, no surprise to God; it came as part of the divine plan for their two young lives. Hence we know it was not a calamity to either. The years of love had their part in the building up of the character and the culture of the spirit of him who was called to higher service. He is the better servant of his Master now in the bright fields where he is, for the enriching of his life which that sweet love wrought in him. She who was left has also received from the experiences of love an enlargement and a culture of heart, by which she has been fitted for gentler and more effective ministry in this world. Then the sorrow through which she has passed has also had its influence upon her life, anointing her for yet holier and more helpful service.

She is not the girl she was in those light-hearted days when the two used to walk and talk together while love's dreams were so bright. It is not long since; but in the little time she has learned strange lessons — lessons which have gone deep into her soul. All life has been changed for her, and in her too. She is a woman now, set apart by the baptism of sorrow. The light still shines in her face; but it is not morning light now, it is the serious light of the midday. She has new joy now — joy which is sorrow transfigured, glorified. God's comfort is in her heart, and a holy peace is in her eyes. She has experienced sore loss, but she never was so rich as she is now.

"What can the brown earth do,
Drenched and dripping through,
To the heart, and dazzled by the sight
Of the light
That cometh after rain?

What can the hurt life do,
Healing through and through,
Caught and captured by the slow increase
Of the peace
That cometh after pain?

I would not miss the flower
Budded in the shower
That lives to lighten all the wealthy scene
Where rain has been,
That blossoms after pain!"

This bereft child need not think of her lifework as in any real sense broken up by the sorrow which has brought such disappointment. It is still God's plan for her that is going on amid the desolation of her hopes. Her friend's work in this world was finished when he passed over to take up new and holier service; but her work is yet here, and she must not lose an hour even for sorrow. Her grief was but an incident in her life; and she must not allow her spirit to be broken by it, or her serving of Christ to be hindered. With heart made more tender by the pain, with hand made more gentle, with sympathy deepened and her whole nature enriched, she is ready to go out now to be a blessing to many. God will care for her life, that no sweet hope of her heart may perish, but that in some other way than she had dreamed of, every holy vision of her love shall yet come true.

> "Strange, strange for thee and me,
>   Sadly afar;
> Thou safe beyond, above,
>   I 'neath the star;
> Thou where flowers deathless spring,
>   I where they fade;
> Thou in God's paradise,
>   I 'neath time's shade!
>
> Strange, strange for thee and me,
>   Loved, loving ever;
> Thou by life's deathless fount,
>   I near death's river;
> Thou winning wisdom's love,
>   I strength to trust;
> Thou 'mid the seraphim,
>   I in the dust."

CHAPTER XXVIII.

LEARNING CONTENTMENT.

NOT many people are contented. Not many seem to think discontent a sin. Not many appear to understand that contentment is a grace which should shine in every Christian character. Yet no grace adds more to the beauty and the comfort of a life than this one. It is also enjoined in the Scriptures as a duty.

The time to get this spirit into our life is in youth. If one has allowed thirty or forty years to pass in discontent and fretfulness, the habit is so firmly rooted that it is almost impossible to change it. But if one begins in childhood to learn to keep sweet in all conditions and circumstances, by the time one has reached maturity the habit has become so much a part of one's very life that it is easy to maintain it.

Contentment does not mean satisfaction with one's attainments. This is a condition which is always unreached, unless it be in some indolent person, one without aspirations and longings. The end of longing is the end of growing.

The great sculptor wept when he found that he had reached his ideal. He saw that that was the end of his progress as an artist.

Contentment, however, is the spirit of restfulness and peace in whatever circumstances one may be placed. St. Paul tells us what it meant in his life, when he says, "I have learned, in whatsoever state I am, therein to be content." The word content means self-sufficing, and implies that he had in his own heart the secret of satisfying, and was not dependent for it on any outside circumstances.

On a dark and stormy night a happy family gathers in the living-room of their home. On the table the lamp burns brightly. About the room the members of the household are grouped. There is gladness, conversation, song, cheer. The household is independent of the outside weather. Beat as the storm may upon the windows, it disturbs not their zest and gladness.

This illustrates the secret of contentment. A true family have it in their own home, in themselves. Paul carried in his heart the secret of peace and of joy, and was not dependent upon circumstances. He wrote this strong sentence in a prison; but the prison atmosphere, hardship, and restraint did not affect his inner life.

Every Christian should have in himself the

same secret. We are God's children, and the strong Son of God is our Saviour and Friend. Our life is hid with Christ in God. Our faith should lift us above the hard experiences of life. We may be in sorrow, but the sorrow should not break the peace. We may have suffering, but the suffering should not destroy the comfort we have in resting in God.

It is not our part to keep ourselves in peace — God's is the keeping; ours is the staying upon God. We are to let ourselves rest down upon God's omnipotence, nestle in the bosom of his everlasting love. We are to stay in the strong, warm refuge, not restlessly tossing ourselves out of it. If we stay in God's love, God will keep us in perfect peace.

We should learn, therefore, to be contented; that is, not to be affected by the things about us; to keep sweet in the most trying experiences, amid trials and annoyances of whatever kind. Living in the midst of cares, we should keep the care out of our heart, having there only the peace of Christ.

It may be of special comfort to young Christians to note that St. Paul says he had *learned* this lesson of contentment. He was quite an old man when he wrote the word, and we may suppose that he was a good many years learning it. Probably it was not an easy lesson for him, and we may suppose that he got it only through long discipline and careful training. At least we are quite sure that it does not come naturally to any one. We have to learn to be contented, and usually it will take us a good while to learn it.

This may seem, therefore, not to be a young person's problem — to be a lesson which the young can scarcely expect to learn. No doubt it should be better learned by the time a Christian reaches mid-life, yet it is not impossible for the young to attain this grace. Contentment is not discontent worn-out, exhausted, fretfulness tired into quiet sleep. Contentment is the peace of God in the heart, diffusing its restful calm through all the life, hushing all its disturbances.

The lesson is set for the young, therefore, for it is in youth that it must be learned. To grow into mid-life or old age discontented is to remain to the end discontented.

If young people realized how lovely the spirit of contentment is, and how unlovely discontent is, they would all strive to learn the lesson, whatever it may cost them. Discontent mars the beauty in the face, makes persons old before their time, makes them petulant, disagreeable, and uncomfortable companions. On the other hand, contentment gives peace, quietness, and simplicity. It makes the face sweet, and puts into the eyes a calm and holy light. It makes one a comfort to others too — a benediction. We all know how much discomfort a fretful person produces in a home or in any association, and how a contented person diffuses cheer and pleasure everywhere. One secret of lovableness is a sweet spirit, restful, at peace, quiet, and undisturbed in any circumstances. We all admire such a person.

Shall we not set this lesson for ourselves in the bright days of youth when we are learning to live? Let us trust God and do our duty, committing all the tangles and frets to him. He will take care of us. Though we must walk through dark ways, we shall always find light; for he who is the Light of the world will walk with us.

It is a great thing to have in one's heart a fountain which will supply all one's needs. Then one can be independent of circumstances and of experiences, and be everywhere and always the same sweet, quiet, rejoicing Christian. Christina Rossetti in one of her exquisite stanzas paints a beautiful picture of the calm and restfulness of the contented soul : —

We never heard her speak in haste;
   Her tones were sweet,
And modulated just so much
   As it was meet.
Her heart sat silent through the noise
   And concourse of the street;
There was no hurry in her hands,
   No hurry in her feet.

Other Solid Ground Titles

In addition to the book in your hand, Solid Ground is honored to offer other uncovered treasure, many for the first time in more than a century:

THE COMMUNICANT'S COMPANION by Matthew Henry
THE CHILD AT HOME by John S.C. Abbott
THE LIFE OF JESUS CHRIST FOR THE YOUNG by Richard Newton
THE KING'S HIGHWAY: *10 Commandments for the Young* by Richard Newton
HEROES OF THE REFORMATION by Richard Newton
FEED MY LAMBS: *Lectures to Children on Vital Subjects* by John Todd
LET THE CANNON BLAZE AWAY by Joseph P. Thompson
THE STILL HOUR: *Communion with God in Prayer* by Austin Phelps
COLLECTED WORKS of James Henley Thornwell (4 vols.)
CALVINISM IN HISTORY *by Nathaniel S. McFetridge*
OPENING SCRIPTURE: *Hermeneutical Manual by Patrick Fairbairn*
THE ASSURANCE OF FAITH *by Louis Berkhof*
THE PASTOR IN THE SICK ROOM *by John D. Wells*
THE BUNYAN OF BROOKLYN: *Life & Sermons of I.S. Spencer*
THE NATIONAL PREACHER: *Sermons from 2nd Great Awakening*
FIRST THINGS: *First Lessons God Taught Mankind* Gardiner Spring
BIBLICAL & THEOLOGICAL STUDIES *by 1912 Faculty of Princeton*
THE POWER OF GOD UNTO SALVATION *by B.B. Warfield*
THE LORD OF GLORY *by B.B. Warfield*
A GENTLEMAN & A SCHOLAR: *Memoir of J.P. Boyce by J. Broadus*
SERMONS TO THE NATURAL MAN *by W.G.T. Shedd*
SERMONS TO THE SPIRITUAL MAN *by W.G.T. Shedd*
HOMILETICS AND PASTORAL THEOLOGY *by W.G.T. Shedd*
A PASTOR'S SKETCHES 1 & 2 *by Ichabod S. Spencer*
THE PREACHER AND HIS MODELS *by James Stalker*
IMAGO CHRISTI: *The Example of Jesus Christ by James Stalker*
LECTURES ON THE HISTORY OF PREACHING *by J. A. Broadus*
THE SHORTER CATECHISM ILLUSTRATED *by John Whitecross*
THE CHURCH MEMBER'S GUIDE *by John Angell James*
THE SUNDAY SCHOOL TEACHER'S GUIDE *by John A. James*
CHRIST IN SONG: *Hymns of Immanuel from All Ages by Philip Schaff*
COME YE APART: *Daily Words from the Four Gospels by J.R. Miller*
DEVOTIONAL LIFE OF THE S.S. TEACHER *by J.R. Miller*

Call us Toll Free at 1-877-666-9469
Send us an e-mail at sgcb@charter.net
Visit us on line at solid-ground-books.com
Uncovering Buried Treasure to the Glory of God

www.ingramcontent.com/pod-product-compliance
Lightning Source LLC
Chambersburg PA
CBHW032111090426
42743CB00007B/320